MORE
MONEY
LESS
HUSTLE

BECOMING THE 7-FIGURE
REAL ESTATE AGENT

MORE
MONEY
LESS
HUSTLE

JSS LENOUVEL

LIONCREST
PUBLISHING

MORE MONEY, LESS HUSTLE

Becoming the 7-Figure Real Estate Agent

ISBN 978-1-5445-2827-4 *Hardcover*
     978-1-5445-2825-0 *Paperback*
     978-1-5445-2826-7 *Ebook*

To my Mom.

You are everything.

CONTENTS

A GIFT FOR YOU

As a complement to this book, my team and I have put together a free resource for you—a course called *The 7-Figure Agent Starter Kit*. It contains trainings, worksheets, and guides that will help you on your journey to becoming a 7-figure real estate agent.

You can get the course at thelistingslab.com/7fa.

Sign up now so that you can work through the material as you go.

INTRODUCTION

The Spaghetti Incident

Two hundred and fifty.

That's how many leads I had to call that day. Good problem to have, right?

Wrong.

Before I tell you why, let me set the stage.

My husband Yves and I had started a real estate business together, and business was good. I was hunkered down in my dungeon of an office (the window was blocked by a huge billboard), the fluorescent lights overhead buzzing away. I had three computer monitors running at the same time, tracking leads from my CRM and going through my calendar and emails like a day trader. My phone headset felt fused to my head as my day had been nothing but cold-calling cold lead after lead.

You can imagine how often I was hung up on. People yelled at me. They even swore. Sure, sometimes, I was lucky enough to book an actual appointment, but they were few and far between. My poor success rate didn't stop me, though. In fact, it made me even more focused and determined to call every lead on that list. Before I knew it, I had forgotten to eat lunch. There was nothing but coffee in my veins.

One of the leads who didn't hang up said they were at work and asked if I could call them back at seven that evening. I checked my calendar, and that's when my heart dropped into my stomach.

Yves and I had a date night scheduled for seven. I had totally forgotten.

Instead of saying no right away, I told myself, *Maybe I can swing the call.* We'd just get to dinner a little later than planned. Then that other voice in my head—the angel—told me, *No! You need boundaries.* That voice was louder—but only a bit.

"I'm sorry, but I'm not available at seven," I said. "Can I call you back tomorrow?"

I heard the response I expected: "I don't know. I'll get back to you." There was no doubt that I'd lost them. But I'd drawn a line in the sand for myself, and it felt good.

Sort of.

After we hung up, I sent a text to Yves, whose office was just down the hall from mine. I asked him if he'd made a reservation for our date night (as if I'd never forgotten about it). He said yes, and that he was so excited to get to spend some "real" time with me.

At this point, I should probably tell you that Yves and I are not your average couple. We are literally obsessed with each other. We tell each other all the time that we are the best thing that's ever happened to each other, and we do everything together.

But our date was *not* the most important thing on my calendar. Not only that, but even when I remembered the date, I wasn't excited like Yves was.

Instead, I felt stressed about the lost time. I knew how I was going to feel when I couldn't answer my phone or respond to messages. After all, what happens when you call 250 people during the day and leave at least a hundred voice messages? The interested leads call you back when their workday is done—when I was supposed to be sitting down to dinner with my husband.

That night, Yves dropped me at the front door of the restaurant and drove off to park. As soon as he pulled away from the curb, I checked my messages and responded to what I could, getting as much done as possible before he came back. When I saw him, I guiltily dropped the phone by my side, hiding it from him. Even if he hadn't seen it (which I'm sure he had), he knew what I was up to. Unfortunately, this was the norm. I was always on my phone, always half there. I'd lost count of the times he'd ask me a question when I was head down, scrolling the screen, with no clue what he'd just said. Yves was always sweet and laughed it off, but I knew there was nothing funny about any of it.

The hostess seated us, and I put my phone face down next to me on the table. We ordered sparkling water and spaghetti bolognese. My smartwatch buzzed with notifications. I counted the missed messages to myself. All I wanted to do was look at my watch and pick up my phone. With each buzz, my stress level went up. I remembered advice from a friend in the industry that every missed call could mean $10,000 out of my pocket. That scarcity mindset made my blood pressure rise by the minute.

Yves, bless him, seemed not to notice. He talked about the vision of our company, about what we were working so hard to build, and about how we needed and deserved a vacation. I wanted to join in his excitement, but I couldn't. I was too distracted.

Our main course came, and we dove in. Of course, because we were eating, we didn't talk as much. Then it happened—a different kind of buzz on my watch. Not a message. A phone call.

Without thinking, I spit my mouthful of spaghetti into my cloth napkin. Then I picked up my phone and, with no explanation, walked out of the restaurant without even a look back at Yves.

Outside, I answered the call—a completely useless lead. They'd seen that I had called earlier in the day but didn't bother listening to the voicemail and called me back directly. They weren't interested in an appointment at all.

I stepped back into the restaurant, and before Yves could see me, I watched him. I looked at his face. He looked miserable, as though someone had punched him in the gut. The man who had stood beside me, who had tolerated my lack of focus and presence in our relationship with kindness and a smile, sat there alone. On our date night.

Oh my God. What have I done?

When I came back to the table, Yves had completely pulled back. Who could blame him? In the middle of a heart-to-heart about our future, I had walked out. Ashamed, I sat back down, facing his disappointment and a napkin full of disgusting chewed-up spaghetti.

And just like that, a switch flipped.

The point of this business was for Yves and me to work together to create the life we wanted. I knew then and there that if I continued on this path, I was putting all of that at risk. We'd been married for almost three years, and we were still supposed to be in the honeymoon phase of our life together. I became super aware of how screwed up my priorities had been. The whole point of our business was to work hard and enjoy the benefits of that work. If we ended up divorced, what was it all for?

I'm as stubborn as they come. I don't like being wrong and will defend myself until I'm blue in the face—but there was no denying that I was absolutely wrong in this situation. I looked Yves in the eye.

"I'm so sorry," I said.

He smiled weakly and said, "Yeah, well, I'm used to it now."

YOU CAN'T POUR FROM AN EMPTY CUP

Yves and I have a storybook love affair, and I wake up each morning grateful that I married such an incredible man who is my partner in both business and life.

Yet that love didn't stop me from leaving him at the table with a napkin full of chewed-up food.

How did I get to that place?

An even more important question—how did *you* get there?

Every time I tell this story to other real estate agents, they nod their heads before I even get to the part where I spit out my food. I'm willing to bet you did the same thing when you read about my distracted date night. The story feels familiar no matter where you were when you realized you'd built yourself a nightmare—and you never forget it.

How many times have *you* been in a situation where you wished you'd made a different choice? Maybe it was your kid's birthday, your anniversary, a date night, or just a conversation you weren't truly present for.

How many times have you looked back and told yourself that you could—and *should*—have done better?

Most of us got into the real estate business believing it has unlimited potential—that there's no ceiling. You can set your own schedule. You're in charge of your life. But you end up in this place where you have no control over either life or your schedule, with your head constantly bumping that ceiling.

Whether you've been an agent for your entire professional life, or you got into the business as a first, second, or third career, you made that decision based on three ideas.

1. You want unlimited income.

2. You want freedom.

3. You want to have some sort of an impact on other people's lives.

Somewhere along the way, though, you got lost. You got lost working *in* the business rather than working *on* your business. You got lost in the idea that you have to be on call twenty-four hours a day. You *also* got lost in the ego lift that comes along with doing everything yourself (because no one can do it as well as you can), always being available for your clients, and always putting them first.

But if your clients always come before your personal life, you end up constantly trying to pour from an empty cup. If you don't take care of yourself first, your clients, your family, and anything or anyone else that is important to you will never get the best of you.

This all comes from the scarcity mindset—the idea that missing a call means losing that potential client and so on and so on, until you're out of business. So, your solution is to answer *every* call and to do *everything* yourself.

That's not a real business—that's a hustle.

And it's time to make a change.

IT'S NOT YOUR FAULT

The traditional ways of doing things in real estate date back to when the only available tool was a paper MLS.

Now we live in an entirely different world with an entirely different set of opportunities that people—especially those who train real estate agents—are ignoring. Although communications technology and methods have changed drastically, you were taught outdated ones.

It's not that the old ways don't work—they can. But I'll bet you hate them. Not only are they difficult, but they're inefficient and unscalable.

Why would you do anything that takes three hours per day when you could automate it? What else could you do with that time? It could be something that actually matters like serving more clients, going to your kid's hockey game, *or* having an uninterrupted dinner with your significant other.

You're probably spending a ridiculous amount of time:

- Cold calling

- Door knocking

- ► Sending flyers

- ► Networking

- ► Holding open houses

Bet you're nodding your head again, aren't you?

Here's the thing—it's not your fault that you're doing these things. No one has taught you any differently—until now.

This book will teach you how to build a real estate business in the age of the internet and technology products that make you both wildly successful *and* happy.

AND—NOT EITHER/OR

John D. Rockefeller said:

> *"I would rather earn 1 percent of*
> *100 people's efforts than 100 percent*
> *of my own efforts."*

This quote stuck with me, especially after the spaghetti incident, because it was the definition of "work smarter, not harder."

The old way of doing real estate is all about the hustle and grind. It is hammered into you that you have to struggle to be successful. Even my dad used to tell me how proud he was of me because of how hard I hustled.

I had to unlearn that. I still wanted to be successful, but I didn't want to kill myself—or my relationship—to get there. I didn't want to live an "either/or" life—I wanted to live an "and" life, meaning I could have this *and* have that.

You can, too. You don't have to choose between success and the things you love in life. You get to have both.

The first step is to realize that most tactics are a no-go. You need to focus on strategy.

Simply put, strategy means making smart, forward-thinking decisions that help you win without needing to put in a lot of effort. Tactics are the actions you take to solve an immediate problem. By the time those agents actually realize they should have focused on coming up with strategies and putting them in place, they could have been a hundred steps ahead. Instead, they have been distracted by shiny-object syndrome, the biggest obstacle to real estate agent success.

This is not a book of tactics. It's a book of immutable strategies and principles that have worked to scale businesses forever—but they haven't ever been used by or applied to the real estate industry. Having studied these principles independently, I put them to use in my own business practices—and found that they worked.

Whether you're selling food, clothing, or real estate, the fundamental principles of business have been the same since people traded in open-air markets. And they'll never change. What *does* change are the mediums through which those principles—specifically marketing—can be practiced.

In this book, I'll teach you the seven pillars that took me from the treadmill of making hundreds of cold calls a day to an efficient business that earned millions of dollars a year. That business also allowed me to go on vacation for weeks at a time without taking a hit to my income. Every single pillar is rooted in a proven and necessary strategy for the longevity, sustainability, and foundation for your business. This book is not about the quick fix—the strategies are designed to provide you with long-term profitability in a *real* business—not a hustle. The pillars are:

- Marketing

- Mindset

- Clients and the Signature System

- Sales conversations

- Operations

- Team hiring and leadership

- Visioning

These pillars will not only transform your business—they'll transform your life.

It's a big claim, I know, but it's one that I'm confident making—because I was the test subject. And I've helped thousands of agents replicate my success.

I'm sharing what I've learned from personal experience now *because, frankly, no one else is.* There are real estate agents suffering the same pain I was. If I can keep even one person from making the same mistakes and maybe losing someone who is important to them and living with regret, then the effort to write this book will have been worth it.

(In fact, keeping agents from making the same mistakes is the focus of my career these days. That's the reason I evolved into founding and creating The Listings Lab, our marketing and mentorship program to teach agents how to double or triple their incoming business in a year without struggling. I knew I could help agents do the same. So now, instead of working *as* an agent, my team and I work *with* agents.)

I also believe these principles are critical to the survival of our industry.

The real estate profession is under attack, and if the industry doesn't step up, agents are going to become obsolete, replaced by tech companies (you know the ones). Only a smaller number of highly niched experts in certain areas will make it. Only incredibly good marketers and/or people who follow the principles outlined in this book are going to be around in the future. If the industry is going to survive, it needs to change how the public sees, receives, and respects agents. We have to elevate our way of doing business. The public sees real estate agents as used-car salesmen—but agents want to be treated and respected like attorneys.

The truth is that we're neither.

To be treated as we want, we need to stop *acting* like the stereotype of a used-car salesman. But with outdated methods being taught, real estate ads read like bad copy for a used car. It may be true that getting your license can't be equated to graduating law school, but what you do comes with a *massive* responsibility. This is a human-to-human business, and when people buy a house, they make their decisions emotionally before they make them logically.

The old way of real estate is creating an entire generation of burned-out agents, but there is another way, and that's what I'm here to tell you. You can have a life *and* be successful in the real estate industry.

NO SHINY OBJECTS

If you're looking for a book full of quick fixes and shiny objects for you to chase around to make yourself feel busy or to feed your ego, put this book down. It's not for you.

And if you don't want your preconceived notions to be challenged, or if you're not willing to unlearn what you've been told is the recipe for success, don't turn the page. There are *a lot* of people who will feel called out by this book. But I'm not here to coddle anyone.

This book is for the people who actually want to build a scalable, sustainable real estate business that supplies those three things that got you into this business in the first place:

- ▸ Unlimited income

- ▸ Personal freedom

- ▸ Tangible impact

Keep reading if they're what you want—it's as simple as that. I promise you that the ride won't be boring. As I tell everyone I meet, if you can't take a joke and laugh with me along the way, we can't be friends. I am both kind and straightforward in the extreme. If that's your flavor of ice cream, we'll have a good time and you'll make a lot of money by making a big difference in people's lives.

If you're in for the journey, then let's take a deeper dive into the seven pillars, where they come from, and why they're going to work for you.

It's time to start living an "and" life.

Chapter One

WHAT NEEDED
TO CHANGE

Let's go back to the restaurant for a minute.

Yves was used to my preoccupation by that point. I'd gotten up in the middle of a conversation countless times to answer a call, and he always took it in stride. He accepted the way things were—at least I thought he had.

But when I came back to the table this time, the mood was heavy. It was the first time I'd left a conversation where we had been talking about connecting more deeply and making more time for each other.

That heaviness was a wake-up call. I became painfully aware of my lack of boundaries, and of the fact that my habits were just as bad as my decisions. When I spit out my food in my napkin and picked up the phone, it wasn't a decision—it was a reaction. Second nature. I'd made such a habit out of prioritizing leads over everything else that it had become a reflex.

And to some extent, I already knew that. In fact, I had told myself that I was going to make a conscious decision to be less reactive. When I told the lead that I couldn't talk to them at 7pm because of my date with Yves, I thought I was making big strides toward doing just that. Obviously, I was wrong. In that moment, I felt like a huge disappointment—to both of us.

You know that feeling when your parents or someone you care about is mad at you, so you try to overcompensate? That's what I did when I sat back down. I made stupid jokes to get Yves to laugh, purely out of shame and guilt.

And that conversation about our future? There was no going back. We returned to surface-level conversations, and when we were quiet, it was an awkward silence. The dynamic between us had completely changed.

Yves and I were talking about having kids at the time, and I knew I couldn't keep going like this if we were going to make that happen. Our only option would be to have a nanny raise our child. I don't mean this as a judgment against anyone who takes that route; if that works for you, great! But it wasn't what I wanted.

Eventually, I realized the time was *never* going to be right. I was never going to have the lifestyle I wanted or be the person I wanted to be for the people that I loved—not until I changed the actual structure of the way I was doing things.

It was after that dinner when I realized that I couldn't just change my behavior. If I was actually going to get better, I had to change the *business*. That meant resetting it so that I didn't have to be so reactive all the time. I knew there had to be a healthier way to live, and I knew I was smart enough to figure it out. My mom was a real estate agent, and she never missed a single event.

If she could do it, couldn't I?

If I was going to learn how to create a business structure that allowed me to do the things I wanted to do, I was going to have to experiment and research. I started by looking into other industries, ones where people made a lot more money without as much outright effort. I had to look at how they avoided being reactive and then figure out how to modify and customize their strategies to work in the real estate industry.

I was determined to get myself out of the old ways of thinking about real estate. I was never prepared to cold call and door knock and manually prospect. I'm a mega introvert, so speaking to that many people every day exhausts me. It wasn't something I was ever going to enjoy, no matter how much I tried.

I've never been a believer in motivation. If you build a business that's purely based on your own motivation, then you will set yourself up to fail because no human being is motivated every single day. That fact is the reason why so many social media influencers have made millions and millions of dollars teaching all of this "rah rah" motivational nonsense, and pumping people up every day. It's just not how humans work—but we keep trying.

(If you're interested in taking a deeper dive into motivation, pick up *Willpower Doesn't Work* by Benjamin Hardy. You'll be glad you did.)

My answer was to create a business that would keep running on the days when I was sick or on vacation, or I just wanted to spend an afternoon picking apples with my husband. I wanted a business that didn't rely on *me* turning the wheel.

In order to achieve that, I had to start by bringing real estate marketing into the twenty-first century.

ARCHAIC MARKETING

Cold calling, door knocking, and "geo-farming" methods— physically putting yourself in front of people—are the standard methods for maintaining awareness, consistency, and frequency in real estate only because when they were introduced, we had no alternatives.

But now that we have computers that fit in our pockets, those methods no longer make sense. Yet they persist.

In his book *Hook Point: How to Survive in a 3-Second World*, Brendan Kane writes:

> With more than 60 million messages sent out on digital platforms every day, we have an incredible amount of information being sent to us constantly.... In fact, the average person spends eleven hours a day interacting with digital media (including digital video, audio, TV, newspapers, magazines, etc.) and scrolls through 300 feet of content. People use their phones 1,500 times a week and check their email in-boxes thirty times an hour. Every sixty seconds on Facebook, there are 400 new users, 317 status updates, 147,000 uploaded photos, and 54,000 shared links. Approximately 95 million photos and videos are shared on Instagram on a daily basis.

So why are real estate agents sticking to the old way of doing things? Buckle up, because you might not like the answer.

Many of the agents who were successful in the 70s, 80s, and early 90s with those old tactics are now broker-owners teaching their agents what they learned way back when. They're not marketers, and they're certainly not up to date.

That old way has *got* to go.

Today, there is so much software available that can automate the tasks you've been doing manually—and that technology should come before you hire another person because it's so much more efficient.

The real estate industry is being challenged by tech companies and iBuyers. In response, agents are throwing their hands up and getting angry without actually doing anything about it. You don't get to choose not to adapt and then get angry when you're replaced.

SERVING EVERYONE VERSUS NICHING DOWN

You can have a neighborhood that has upsizers, downsizers, first-time Buyers, and investors, all in one postal or zip code. If you're using the older methods of marketing—say flyers, for example—your messaging has to be incredibly broad. All you end up doing is getting an impression in front of someone for the sake of an impression.

It's really important that each agent niches down, which is choosing a group of ideal clients and customizing your marketing to attract them. Then we're able to use targeted online advertising (something we'll discuss in depth later in the book), and we look at the human component. You understand the psychology of the client's life transition. You look at what's going on in a client's head during their next real estate transaction. And you use that to create incredibly targeted messaging.

Now, you may have read other real estate books that say you should get in front of as many eyeballs as possible—to paint with the widest brush instead of narrowing down to a specific market. But when you do that, you get filtered out as noise.

The riches are in the niches, and specificity wins—every time. You probably wouldn't trust your family doctors to install a pacemaker in your chest. Your clients also don't want a generalist; they want someone who specializes in what they need.

We're at a point now where *everyone* seems to have a real estate license. Effective marketing means being able to articulate what's in the back of someone's mind better than they can—sometimes even *before* they can. You cannot do that if you're painting with a broad brush. There's a reason that the best commercials make us cry. The key to good marketing, the key to mental market share, is emotion—building "know, like, and trust" through sound psychology and messaging targeted to a specific group.

Make no mistake—if you're still trying to use vague, nonsensical taglines, at some point you will disappear. You will become irrelevant.

People don't move because it's fun. They move because something in their life isn't serving them and they're trying to solve that problem with a different space. It could be that they need a new location, a bigger or smaller space, or a neighborhood that better fits their lifestyle. Whatever their reasons, creating messaging that will resonate with their *actual* needs and wants will be far more powerful than a generic flyer or advertisement.

Most real estate advertising is ridiculous because agents lean on "I'm number one!" messaging. They focus the attention on themselves—not their potential clients—because they can't actually create marketing that will truly strike a chord with people.

But people don't care about you. They care about themselves.

Hearing you talk about how great you are or how many awards you've won doesn't solve your ideal client's problem—that they're terrified they won't be able to find a house before their move-out date or that their marriage won't actually survive the time it takes to find said house.

RELATIONSHIP SCALING

There's a reason why the CEOs of huge companies become celebrities—Tesla has Elon Musk, and Apple had Steve Jobs. People need a face behind the brand. In so many of today's large businesses, consumer trust is starting to fade, if not disappear altogether, so companies bring in a face and work to build trust in it.

Building trust is building a relationship. You can't just hide behind a logo anymore, especially in real estate. This is a human-to-human business, so it's important that people get to know, like, and trust you. People create comfort with other human beings, and it's not by being perfect. Perfection is boring, and it makes other people feel inadequate. People build connections through vulnerability and story. We have to break down barriers to trust.

There are two types of celebrities. One is very approachable; the other is not. If you saw Brad Pitt walking down the street, you probably wouldn't feel comfortable walking up to him and giving him a high five.

But there are certain influencers that most people would have no problem approaching to say hello. Yes, they're "celebrities," but people feel like they already know them because they've been following their story on their social media accounts and feel like they're part of their lives. It's like when an actor breaks the fourth wall in a movie and talks to the audience. That's approachability, and it's what you need to build with your client audience.

You don't need to create an image of perfection, screaming about how you're the top real estate agent around. People don't care about that. What they do care about is that *you* care about and understand *them*.

That's part of what you can demonstrate with psychologically driven marketing content.

Let's say you're serving "upsizers." These are mostly young families and people who have outgrown their first space. You need to show that you truly understand their pains, problems, fears, and desires. There is the emotion of letting go of the first home they bought, the house that their kids were born in. But there's also the frustration of fighting every day because they're tripping over the kids' toys, and everyone is sharing the same bathroom. And, of course, there are the financial worries that come along with moving into a bigger home.

But most agents come at these situations purely from a numbers standpoint. As a result, the clients don't feel understood. Worse yet, they feel like they're just another deal or transaction for that agent. In fact, I advise you to take the words *transaction* and *deal* out of your marketing copy altogether.

A sale is a transaction or deal for *you*—not for the client. Don't decide for the client what a sale is for them. Do your research and find out what language your market is using. Speak to them in *their* words and language, not yours.

Real estate agents' failure to do this is why the tech real estate companies like Zillow and Redfin have become a threat to our profession. So many agents have become so generalized that they're not providing a specialized, customized, high-value service. When that happens, the public doesn't value what we do. They think all they need is someone to throw their home up on the MLS and to send them the paperwork. Who wouldn't pay a lot less to do that?

The market dictates what constitutes value. You can be the best copywriter in the world, but you cannot create desire in a marketplace; you can only reflect it. The right messaging comes from the market. But far too many agents create their marketing—along with everything else in their business—in a vacuum of:

Who do I want to be? What do I want to look like?

The truth is that your entire business should be built upon solving a particular problem for a particular type of person. Everything about your marketing, your messaging, your service package—all of it—should come from figuring out what solution your client needs. Your potential clients could not care less about who you want to be or how you want to look. If you want to survive in this industry, now is the time for an ego check.

STOP HUSTLING.
STOP GRINDING.

The hustle-and-grind mentality is not sustainable. Period.

We have an epidemic of burnt-out real estate agents, which hurts not only them, but also the industry. People enter and leave it in a steady churn, without ever doing a great deal of business because their businesses rely on consistent hard work, motivation, and grinding every day. Real estate is still very much built upon a jungle-gorilla chest-beating mindset of hurting yourself to create wins. The idea is that if you want to be successful, you have to suffer.

Stick with this mentality and you'll end up becoming a martyr to your friends, family, and business. Is that why you got into real estate? Is that the picture you painted in your head that inspired you to get your license?

What do you actually *want*? What do you want your life to look like? It sounds cliché, but when you're lying on your deathbed, are you going to be super glad that you made two hundred phone calls per day when you could have been spending time with your loved ones? Almost without fail, every older person you speak to toward the end of their life says they wish they had worked less.

There's a reason you chose to run your own business. You didn't want to work sixteen hours a day for someone else—so why would you want to do the same when you're working for yourself? You wanted more control and more freedom.

I've spent literally millions of dollars testing the strategies I'm presenting in this book. They are the identical strategies I used to change my mindset and overhaul my business. At The Listings Lab, I've already taught them to thousands of other agents who've repeated my results.

But before they can work for you, you need to open to shifting how you think about this business and shed that hustle-and-grind legacy mindset.

YOU WILL BE CHALLENGED

It's unfortunate, but it's true.

Everyone has a different set of problems that will stop them from growing their business—but all real estate agents have similar core patterns that create business growth. Knowing that, realize that you will be challenged by at least one—if not more—of the pillars necessary to creating a seven-figure business.

You'll run into challenges because at least one of the things these pillars address is broken in your business, and it's causing a bottleneck. You might already be making seven figures, but you have zero freedom. You might have freedom, but you're not making consistent money and are nowhere near a seven-figure income. You can hustle to seven figures, but at some point, *you* will become the bottleneck, and you *will* burn out. It's not until you have all of the pillars dialed in that you begin to experience smooth sailing.

And I do mean *all* the pillars. This cannot be a piecemeal approach. You can't just apply one of the strategies to your business and think it will fix your issues. Every single one of these pillars works in conjunction with the others.

When I implemented these strategies in my business after the spaghetti incident, it took me about six months to see the changes. In the end, these strategies not only turned around my business; they turned around my life.

I had a lot more clarity in terms of who I wanted to be and what I wanted to do. My priorities became my friends, my family, and especially my husband. I became a nicer person. I was more trusting. I was nicer to be around. I wasn't stressed out all of the time. I started looking at my life through the lens of what I wanted—because I had the space and freedom to do so—instead of what was expected of me.

When you get to a point in your life where money's not an issue anymore—when you're not chasing it, you're not constantly clouded by scarcity and fear. Things become very clear.

I don't bring my phone with me to date nights anymore. My husband and I have long conversations. We're again completely obsessed with each other.

I also want for you that freedom, that clarity, that sense of abundance instead of scarcity.

But before you can have it, there's work to be done, and that work starts in the next chapter, where we take a deep dive into the first pillar: marketing.

Chapter Two

PILLAR ONE:
MARKETING

I got my license through a large, well-known training brokerage (I won't say names, but you can probably guess). One of the first things they required of me was to take the DiSC Personality Profile. I didn't know what to expect, but what I did already know was that I was—and am—very introverted. But I figured they were going to use the results to help me figure out how best to run my business.

That was not the case.

Instead, they interpreted the results to say that I was not a "dominant profile," and therefore not fit to lead a team. That's hilarious considering the work I do now and what I've built, but there was nothing funny about it at the time.

I'm not saying this is the test's fault. But I was disheartened. I thought that maybe I misunderstood what I believed to be my potential. The result created this feeling of disappointment, not in the test, or even the people at the brokerage that interpreted the results that way. I was disappointed in myself.

But in addition to being an introvert, I'm also incredibly stubborn; you'll probably hear me say it again. I think you need to be stubborn to make the kinds of changes we're talking about. So, I didn't sit wallowing in my disappointment for long. In fact, the profile results were motivation for me to prove them wrong. I had to figure out how to do things my own way.

I made the incorrect assumption that my brokerage was responsible for providing me with all the tools to be successful, but that's not the business a brokerage is in. (I realize now that few agents realize that.)

I went on that assumption—and I hated every second of it. I would knock on a door and immediately hope that no one answered, just so I could go back to the brokerage and tell them I did X many house-visits that day. I didn't know what else to do, and so I followed it until I was spitting out my spaghetti in front of my husband on our date night. I knew that if I didn't figure out another way to generate leads that I wasn't going to last long—if at all—in this business.

Then I had kind of a "duh" moment. I realized there was one person I'd seen who never followed any of these methods—my mom. She'd never done any of the things this brokerage wanted to teach me.

What she *did* was relationships. Her business was 100 percent relationship-based. Could mine be too? Well, I knew how to have conversations, but being an introvert, I wasn't the person to go to networking events or parties, hand out my card, and shoot the shit with strangers.

And even though I was in my twenties, I was often mistaken for a teenager, so I also struggled with the fact that every person who met me assumed I was inexperienced. I learned my stuff backwards and forwards so I could impress potential clients and make them forget about how old I looked.

Right around this time—and I'm going to date myself here—I learned about a brand-new thing called Facebook.

PROSPECTING IN MY PJS

I started combing through Facebook Marketplace and having online conversations with people I found there. What better way for an introvert to talk to a stranger than through a computer? I searched for people looking for houses or rentals and sent them direct messages.

That was how I started to build my business—sitting at my laptop, prospecting in my pajamas. There I was comfortable meeting people, booking appointments, and only later conducting business with them in person.

At the time, I was doing something that practically no one else was. I was using technology in an industry that didn't—and frankly still doesn't—use it well, at least not in the ways they could or should. It made me so efficient that I was able to talk with so many more prospective clients than if I were out beating the streets.

I wanted to know more.

I got a job working for a builder so I could learn the residential real estate business. To understand every angle—resale, preconstruction outside sales, and inside sales—I went to every single marketing meeting.

What I learned is that even the builders were marketing in an outdated way. Instead of running ads online, they were spending $10,000 on a one-page ad in a newspaper. A *newspaper*. And the ad was ridiculous. There was no addressing the potential buyer for the project. Instead, they generally featured a picture of a pretty girl coming out of a swimming pool—completely old school and, frankly, cringeworthy. Sadly, you'll see many of those kinds of ads to this day.

By studying how other industries marketed, I realized that none of their successful techniques had any parallels in the real estate industry. No one in our business was doing what other sectors were doing—despite the fact that what they were doing could be applied to real estate. I just had to figure out *how*.

So, I started a long evolution of testing, running ads, and creating landing pages. I can't honestly tell you how much I've spent testing and running Google and Facebook ads, but I can tell you it was *a lot*. But I wanted to be ahead of the curve, and that was going to mean spending some money to make some money.

We now use a methodology that is broken down into three pieces:

- Relevancy

- Omnipresence

- Intimacy

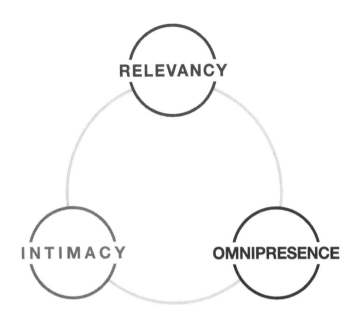

Relevancy

When someone even begins to think about buying or selling a home, they go into what is called "discovery mode." When they're in that state, if you don't create a relevant marketing message to put in front of them, you'll get filtered out as noise. There are a million agents out there, all saying, "Look at me, look at me! I'm number one!" The only way you'll break through that noise is with messaging tailored to the client's needs and wants. Relevant messaging gets your foot in the door.

There are four pieces to Relevancy:

1. Services

2. Messaging

3. Positioning

4. Niche

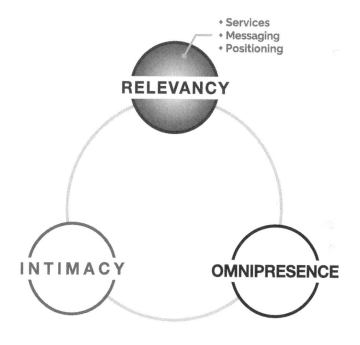

Services are exactly what they sound like—they're what you actually do. They're your methodology or process for getting people the results they're looking for. This is customized as your Signature

System (something we'll visit in-depth later on). Customize your Signature System based on where someone is in the process and what their needs are.

The *Messaging* is how you describe your services. What do you actually do for your prospect, and how will they ultimately benefit from working with you?

Your *Positioning* is how you set yourself apart from the competition. What makes you special? What is your unique value proposition?

For example, towards the end of my days as a real estate agent, one of my advantages was that I had established strong relationships with builders. That meant I always had priority access to new properties coming to the market. From a value proposition standpoint, I knew my markets so well that I was able to tell anyone the price per square foot for every condominium in the city off the top of my head. I could do the same with maintenance and HOA fees. That information was always immediately accessible. That's an example of how you want to find the extra layer of value that's customized to your clients' needs as opposed to just generic stuff.

Communicating these things about my services, messaging, and positioning to prospects made me extremely relevant in their eyes.

However, you can't be relevant to everyone. As the saying goes, if you try to speak to everyone, you speak to no one. When we talk about Relevancy, part of that conversation has to include *Niching* down, or speaking to a specific target demographic.

The old school way of niching down was doing it in terms of location. The effective way is in terms of life transition. Niche down to the *human* to create messaging that truly resonates. That's how you break through the noise.

Everyone who is moving—from a residential standpoint—is moving because of a life transition or a problem in their current situation that they believe can be solved with a move. So, instead of niching down in terms of townhouses, niche down in terms of upsizers or downsizers, first-time Buyers, etc.

A Note about Niching Down

One of the biggest mistakes I've seen people make is going after multiple niches at once. You know the saying about being good at everything but great at nothing? It applies here as well.

Start with one niche and dominate it. Once you have, you can move on to another. Remember, the riches are in the niches.

From a marketing standpoint, the worst tagline you can use is "I'm here for all of your real estate needs." That immediately gives a sense of desperation and lack of specialization. It's as if you're saying, "I'll take what I can get."

The key to drawing someone in is specific, psychology-based messaging. This can only be done well if it's directed to one demographic.

Though being so specialized might go against everything you've ever taught—get over it. The narrower your focus, the more successful you'll be.

When you're relevant to people, you don't need to "spray and pray" (spray the area with your face and number, and pray somebody calls you) with your marketing. They'll listen (and tell their friends) because you're speaking directly to them about the problems they're having. "Have you bugged my house?" is a question you should be hearing regularly; if no one's asking you that question . . . it's because you're not relevant to them.

Omnipresence

Once we actually know who this target demographic is, you should appear to be *everywhere* to them.

Omnipresence is when you literally appear—or at least seem to appear—everywhere in your prospect's life. You dominate their screen. There are three components to this concept.

1. Timing

2. Frequency

3. Platform

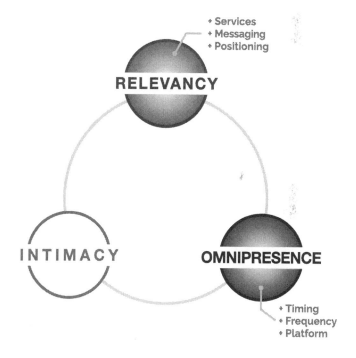

The goal of marketing is always to be in the right place at the right time. What you're doing is getting your messaging in front of people so consistently and so frequently that, in your client's eyes, you feel like their only choice to get the help they need to buy or sell their home.

You want to be top of mind at all times. You're not just appearing out of the blue when they're trying to make a decision. You're showing up, offering value, and building a relationship so that by the time they are actually ready to make a transition, you're the only person who has actually spoken to their specific problems, fears, and desires. That's how you eliminate competition, commission haggling, and clients who think of you as a glorified doorman.

For the most part, this is done online. You show up everywhere your prospects go online, to the point that they see you two to five times a day. This is done through targeting, retargeting, organic social media, and email.

Have you ever gone on Amazon and clicked on, for example, a pool table, and then all you see on every other site you visit for the next two weeks are pool tables? That happens because you've been "pixeled," so that business can now follow you around the internet.

We then use the same method—retargeting people with various types of psychological content to take someone from stranger to client with automation—sending the right message, to the right person, at the right time, on the right platform. This gets people to build that "know, like, and trust" factor with you without ever realizing it.

(To be clear—there is a textbook's worth of material on how to do this, and it goes beyond the scope of this book. In the conclusion, I'll link you to a free training that can start you on this path. For now, focus on embedding the concept of Omnipresence into your marketing strategy—then focus on the "how.")

Traditional methods, including geo-farming, are outdated means of Omnipresence. Sure, they're ways to stay top of mind, but they're not targeted. It all goes back to basic psychology. The human brain is said to be able to quickly remember only two names in any industry.

Don't believe me? Close your eyes and tell me two brands of sneakers.

Ninety-nine percent of the people who read this book are going to say "Nike" and "Adidas." Why? Because those brands are *omnipresent*. You want to achieve that same effect in your prospect's market. You want to be the first person they think of when it comes to real estate.

Omnipresence also builds trust through something called the mere exposure effect. When the human brain is exposed to the same person over and over again, we build trust with that person.

While it's a horrible example, this is closely related to Stockholm Syndrome (about people bonding with their captives). That this condition exists might point to a broken psychological aspect of humans, but there you have it.

We also build trust by giving before we ask anything or serving before we sell. You would never walk up to a complete stranger on the street and ask them for something (unless you were having an emergency), would you? But almost all of today's real estate marketing asks for something—"Call me"—before the agent has given anything more than a picture of their head.

Being omnipresent means you give value over and over again so that when you do eventually ask for something, it doesn't feel like such a hard ask. The element of reciprocity is already there. The kind of value that you give will also depend on your niche. What do they need to hear from you (not what do you want to say)?

Finally, Omnipresence also works so well because of what I call the "halo of success." People usually want to work with those who are trusted and successful. So, here's an example:

Let's say that "Sally" sees "John," the real estate agent, two to five times per day online. She'll assume that everyone in the entire market is also seeing John that much. She'll probably even think, "Wow, he runs a lot of ads. He's everywhere. He must be spending a fortune. If he's spending that much money, then the ads must be working. If the ads are working, he must be really successful, and he must be the person I should talk to."

What Sally doesn't realize is that John is placing those ads in front of the people who are relevant. It's a much smaller audience than just everyone, and retargeting is actually very cheap to do. It's the big fish/small pond effect—and it can work *quickly*. You can become the authority in that niche practically overnight.

The platform you choose is also super important. For most savvy agents, Omnipresence starts with retargeting on Facebook. But that's just one channel. You can also use YouTube, email ad networks, Instagram, Google, and LinkedIn—they're all channels where you can show up for your audience.

Omnipresence is about concentrating a good portion of your advertising on someone after they've become a lead. Doing so gives you a much better chance of converting that lead to a client. Take a small number of leads and increase your Relevancy by being in front of them with the right timing and the right frequency on the right platform.

— what is the market saying?

• Data Analysis ♀

But first you have to get out there and do the market research because your messaging cannot come from you. The messaging *has* to come from the market itself. The larger companies of the world aren't going out and interviewing their ideal client's profile. They're creating generic messaging to work from Texas to Florida to Chicago. They make the message as vanilla as possible so they can say that it will make sense no matter where people see it.

But that doesn't work in real estate. Aim for everyone, hit no one.

And when you actually niche down and get the messaging tight? That's when marketing becomes really, really easy.

Figuring this out meant that I no longer had to be the stock broker wannabe with multiple screens, a headset, and my CRM open all day. Instead of having to chase, people were now coming to me. This is, by the way, also how we bring people into our ecosystem in The Listings Lab. Every person who comes into one of our programs is a living, breathing testament to the power of Omnipresence.

Intimacy

Intimacy is entirely focused on creating authentic, deep-feeling relationships with your potential clients.

Most consumers feel like a lot of industries are highly automated and impersonal. That's not to say automation isn't important. It allows for progress on a larger scale. But the most critical thing in any business is people—and people are dying for human connection, especially online.

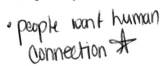

Unfortunately, most real estate marketing isn't about actually helping people or building that deeper layer of trust. Agents just want to talk to anyone who will listen. When you shift the focus to Intimacy or conversation, especially with the people in your audience, you end up with great relationships—at scale. Once again, there are three major components to Intimacy:

1. Connection

2. Conversation

3. Community

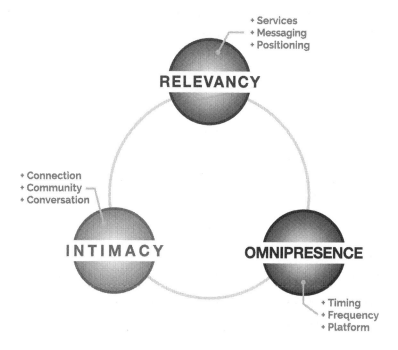

Connection comes down to being honest and authentic. This is not about putting on the perfect show. This isn't about pretending. Perfection is boring, especially online. It's just procrastination in a cuter outfit. Nothing is ever perfect. Strive instead for *done*. Take messy action.

If you're sitting at home in your pajamas, show up sitting at home in your pajamas. Be yourself and show a wide range of realness and authenticity. ← Not sure about this

Connection means being open and vulnerable, sharing things you've gone through, showing people that you're a real person who fosters better and deeper relationships. You do this by telling personal stories and talking about your beliefs. •

Who am I what are my beliefs?

This doesn't mean you *have* to, but it also means you *can*. When I was interviewed for *Entrepreneur* magazine, I let it all hang out. I was open about some of the uglier things in my life that led me to where I am today. I ended up with more business as a direct result of that interview than from anything else I've ever done. Our members have talked about being homeless as kids, leaving abusive relationships, getting divorced, having PTSD, losing a loved one, and other real parts of their lives.

Understandably, you might be hesitant to do this, but when it comes to creating a connection, being open and vulnerable with your audience works like magic. It creates trust. It breaks down the wall. Potential clients no longer see you as someone who might scam them because you have a story, and you're willing to share it honestly. You don't have to do it all in one day, either. You can start by sharing at a small level, and working towards revealing more of how you got to where you are.

Conversations are one of the few pieces of your business that can't be automated. You can and should take the time to actually talk to the people who make up your audience. So many agents who run ads don't take the time to even reply to comments. You *have* to be a part of the conversation. Respond to emails and promote conversation and discussions in your Facebook community. Dig a little deeper and get to know your audience.

Community, then, is *not* just about having a big Facebook group or large following but creating a safe space in an online forum for people to get to know and support each other as human beings. It's about creating a tribe. I would rather have a thousand people who absolutely love me, than a hundred thousand people who kinda like me.

When I was willing to open up and share more about myself, people felt like they owed me a piece of themselves. The conversations I was having with clients went from transactional to personal; they were trusting me with some of the most important details of their lives. When you lead with Intimacy, your clients will follow and everyone will be the better for it. You'll know how to solve their problems, and they'll know they're dealing with someone who understands them. That's a kind of emotional resonance that a bus bench or billboard can never get you.

THE SUM IS GREATER THAN THE PARTS

So how does all of this work together?

First, realize that these ideas *do* all work together. You can't just implement one or two of these things. You might already have a few down pat and see some successes here and there. But you only achieve the power of the compound effect when you perform all of these strategies together. Only then will you see consistent success.

You can't spend your time and money only to become omnipresent. For example, when is the last time you saw an ad for an agent on the side of a bus shelter? If you're in the industry, you'd pay attention to it. But if you were a consumer who wasn't ready to either buy or sell, would you even look at the ad? Of course not. This is what it means to have no relevance to or Intimacy with your audience.

You're physically omnipresent to some people if you have an ad on every corner—but who cares? Who wants to make potentially the biggest investment of their life with someone with whom they have no relationship?

If you're only omnipresent but not relevant or intimate, you become a mosquito. People can't get away from you, and you annoy them.

So many agents fall into this category. They're constantly shoving their listings in people's faces and talking about their success. Meanwhile, they're not telling their clients anything about themselves. People have no idea what they stand for, what they specialize in, or why they should care about either of those things. They're also not giving any real value. Most agents just follow what other agents are doing. They see another agent doing it and think they're supposed to do the same thing.

Now, what happens if you're only intimate but not relevant or omnipresent? You end up in the business "friend zone." You become that agent who's great to hang out with, but who no one would actually buy anything from. You make great connections, have great conversations, and build a terrific community—but if you don't have a relevant message that you're omnipresent with, you're just someone nice to have around, not worth taking seriously in business.

If you've ever been disappointed or angry that a friend or family member uses someone else as an agent…*this* is why. People won't put what is likely their biggest investment in the hands of someone they don't think is a competent expert in their field. That's true even if you shared a bedroom for a decade or lived next door to them for fifteen years. Yes, you're intimate, but you're not relevant or omnipresent to them.

When you're relevant to someone *and* omnipresent, you've turned into an authority in that client's life. You're someone who understands their struggles and provides them with solutions, all while regularly showing up and proving that you really know what you're talking about. That's authority.

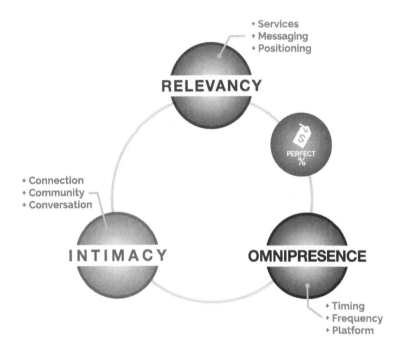

At this point, you're able to charge at the top end of the commission spectrum (something we'll talk about later in the book)

because people see you as an authority—not someone they're going to bargain with.

THE IDEAL CLIENT

When all of these pieces come together, you'll be able to attract your ideal client. To keep from compromising your values, you want to work with people who are as close to a perfect fit with you as possible.

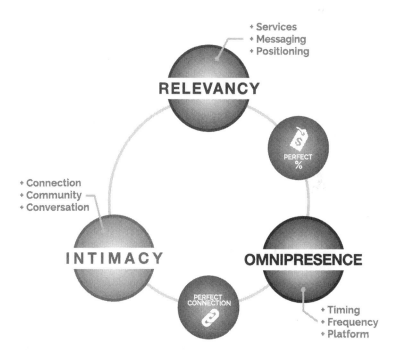

We've all worked with people who *didn't* feel like a good fit—someone who just didn't get you, didn't care about your values, or treated you like any other service provider. It can be a painful and stressful experience. These people waste your time. You put in a ton of work with them and then they end up backing out or selling with someone else.

This happens when you live in scarcity or when you don't have a system in place like the one discussed in this chapter. You take on clients that aren't a good fit because you need the money. But the truth is that you need to love your clients, too.

what type of client who be a good fit?

When you show your audience the real you, when you're open about your values, you draw in those people who resonate with you. The clients who come to you will share those common values, and you'll *actually* have a good time. You'll be excited to work with those clients. You'll want to help them find that perfect property or sell their home.

Who takes on mortgages?
What do I know about mortgages?
What are my values?

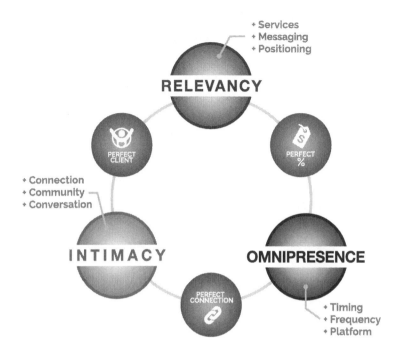

This is the power of all of these ideas put together—the perfect client, the perfect commission, and the perfect connection. *This* is how you explode the growth in your business. This is the compound effect.

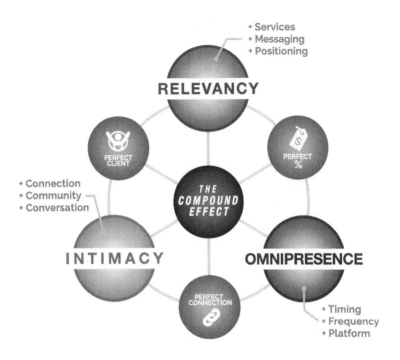

Now, you have a larger and more engaged audience. Consider that larger audience to be insurance for your business because, with it, no matter what happens in the world, your business will be fine.

You will also end up with more social proof. By this, I mean that people will automatically assume authority when they visit your social media presence. That audience of fifty thousand followers automatically infers more authority than an audience of ten. You don't need hundreds of thousands of people to be following you, but you need a critical mass of people who care about the content you're putting out. That proof also gives you a better opportunity to get your message out. Additionally, when you go to hire and grow your team, you'll have more access to people who already know you and understand your message.

While it might seem obvious, this compound effect allows you to do more deals, make more money, and generate more cash flow by charging a full commission. That means no more discounting. If you're reducing your commission, you're doing it because you're competing for people who don't see your value. If someone doesn't want to work with you because you're not willing to discount, you've done something *right*. They're not your ideal client. Let them go.

Finally, the compound effect leads to more meaningful relationships, and not just with your potential clients. Now that you have a thriving business and a growing audience, you have access to more profitable partnerships. You get approached by media outlets, and you can leverage PR. You have a powerful network of referrals. All of this lets you both scale your business and take a higher profit of the income for yourself out of the business.

Again, attraction is at the center of all of this.

When it comes to manual and traditional marketing, you're taught to knock on doors, call people, and chase them down. Even people who are lead-generating online are only collecting a bunch of phone numbers and email addresses. They're still chasing people, just in a different way.

Relevancy, Omnipresence, and Intimacy are not plug and play. You're not going to create a template and throw in a bunch of photos of yourself along with some generic messaging. You're not going to throw up a pre-scheduled stats graphic that forty other agents post on the same day at the same time.

You're going to take things to the next level and redefine what a lead is. A phone number and an email are *not* leads. A real lead is an inbound conversation—someone who is reaching out to say, "Hey, I've seen your stuff, and I'm ready to talk to you about my real estate situation to see if we can work together."

That's attraction. No more chasing. Bring your clients to you.

This concept of marketing has evolved even since I started teaching it to agents because platforms, messaging, and technology change. Initially, I was using landing pages to sell real estate, but we don't use those anymore. Change is inevitable; you must be prepared to evolve. This is why it's so important to be sure that you self-identify as a marketer, not just as an agent.

When I left the builder and began seeing myself as a marketer, I went from essentially zero dollars to seven figures—in six months.

That was with a team of two—me and Yves—while I was the only one doing the selling.

And while it was terrific that I could be that successful as the sole agent, the fact that I was the only one represented a mindset block that I had to change.

Which brings me to the next pillar: mindset.

Chapter Three

PILLAR TWO:
MINDSET

Growing up, I always thought I had to do everything on my own as a lone wolf. I had to be the best at whatever I was going to be, and the one to figure out how to do that. Even when I participated in team sports, at the end of the day, I still felt like it was me against the world.

I was always trying to impress my dad, to make him proud. He was tough on us. His expectations were always sky high. I grew up with a little brother who was—and is—smarter than me, and that was hard as well. I felt like I constantly had to prove myself. The internal pressure to be the best was unbelievably heavy for a kid to carry.

And it made me feel very much alone.

One of my first sports was swimming. It doesn't matter if you're on a relay team or if you're swimming solo—the minute you're in the water, you're on your own. I vividly remember waking up in the middle of the night before meets because I was so anxious about my results. I put so much pressure on myself that I wasn't having any fun.

When I started swimming, I was only ten; my body was still growing. Swimming involves a lot of repetitive motion at the joints, and after only four years of competing, I got badly injured, to the point that my shoulder required surgery. Afterward, I couldn't swim at that same level of competition anymore.

I vividly remember crying outside of the pool changing room. The coach, who had first recruited me to the team, sat next to me. I told her that I didn't know who I was without competing. I felt like it defined me, and I couldn't imagine doing anything else. No thirteen-year-old should feel that way—but there I was. That pressure to be the best and to do things on my own had come to define my identity.

My coach steered me toward rowing, something my shoulder could handle because of the lack of overhead movements. And it was on a team! It was the kind of team where everyone works together, all at once, to achieve a goal—not individuals in the water alone. Surely functioning as part of a team would get rid of my lone-wolf mentality, right?

Wrong.

Crew required that each team member compete individually to earn a seat in the boat. Even when I did make it on the boat, I still felt like I was in constant competition with the other members on my team.

Sadly, that mindset carried over from athletics to academic life. I went to a very cliquey girls' school, and though I was relatively popular, I never felt the need or desire to go where everyone else was going to or to stay close with those friends when it came time for university. There wasn't anything wrong with them—they were all wonderful people. I just felt like I needed my own experience.

When I eventually graduated and went into real estate, I learned a ton from my mom, but I didn't want the optics of people thinking I was riding on her coattails to success. I felt that familiar pressure—both internal and external—to create success on my own.

The freedom real estate offers allowed me to think outside the box for my business. I appreciated the independence I had, but even in the best of times, this is a lonely business. On top of that, I couldn't let go of that old lone-wolf mentality. I was going to make it work.

Until I couldn't anymore.

After a number of years, it all got to be too much. I had too many clients. I know, I know, it sounds like a good problem to have (I call these champagne problems)—until it isn't. I was being pulled in too many directions and trying to do too many things that I wasn't good at. That's how I ended up spitting pasta into a fancy napkin.

I hit an emotional breaking point. Right around the time of the spaghetti incident, Yves and I were sitting in the little condo we were renting. Business was great, and we were making tons of money—but we were still living in this tiny place because we didn't even have time to move. We only had time to run the business.

One evening, my phone rang—and I started to cry. I handed the phone to Yves and told him he had to answer it. Everyone wanted something from me, and I felt like I had nothing left. I had reached a point of extreme burnout.

Something had to change, or something was going to give.

YOUR MINDSET IS YOUR REALITY

Your mindset is the total sum of all your beliefs—and your mindset determines your outcomes. If you believe that you have to suffer to be successful, you're going to end up building something that makes you suffer.

The beautiful thing, though, is that you can change your mindset—and it's not as hard as you might think, because almost everything in your life is entirely in your control. Rather than thinking that life is happening to you, tell yourself that you are creating the life that you have and want. Where you are now, the good and the bad—you created that.

This mindset shift is unbelievably important.

From the beginning of your real estate career, you've been taught that you need to grind. That you have to hustle. That success only comes from huge sacrifice. What happens then is that you never become efficient, and you embody the idea that suffering is a part of success.

But that's just part of the problem.

You have to transition from a mindset of scarcity to one of abundance. This might sound a little woo-woo, but bear with me. If your focus is only on the negative—your bills, your lack of clients, and the slow market, then you'll continue to experience that slowness because it's where your attention and your beliefs are. Justine Faerman at the Flow Consciousness Institute calls this the BETDAR Framework.[1] The simplified version of this notion is that what you believe is the first step to everything that you create.

Beliefs trigger emotions.

Emotions lead to thoughts.

Thoughts create decisions.

Decisions trigger actions.

Actions lead to…

Results.

So, if you believe that the market is slow and it's impossible to be successful without struggle, those negative beliefs will compound, creating a feedback loop. You won't get the results you're looking for because you don't believe they're possible. By believing the

---

[1] Justine Faerman, "Mapping the Evolution of Consciousness: A Holistic Framework for Psychospiritual Development," Flow Consciousness Institute June 11, 2016, https://www.flowconsciousnessinstitute.com/wp-content/uploads/2017/01/Mapping-the-Evolution-of-Consciousness-A-Holistic-Framework-for-Psychospiritual-Development-Ver-2.0.pdf.

market is too slow to create business, you're fulfilling the feedback loop you've created and proving yourself right. You're just confirming your beliefs.

The good news is that you can do the exact same thing with a *positive* thought. You can tell yourself, "Maybe the market is slow, but I believe there is abundance. I believe there is still business to be had. I believe I can find it." Because you believe that, everything you do is going to push you toward that action and result. Now you've created a positive feedback loop because the results will prove your initial belief in your initial thought.

It's like when you're thinking about buying a specific car, and suddenly it seems like everyone on the road is driving that same car. Your mind is wired to make you aware of things. If you want to change what you're aware of, you have to shift what you're thinking about.

THE EGO ACCOUNT

When I went through my period of emotional burnout, I was focused on the lack of time, energy, and space that I had, when the truth was, I had the champagne problem of too much business. But the idea that I had to do everything myself because no one could do it as well as I could kept me from being and feeling supported. I had gotten to the point where I was the bottleneck in my own business. I was trying to prove that I was better and stronger, and that I could suffer more.

You have two accounts you can choose to fill—your bank account or your ego account. I was filling my ego account. Even though that's not what I actually wanted, it filled my ego account to know all these people wanted to work with me.

But the truth is that you can only fill one account. You have to choose. So, which one is it going to be?

Filling your ego account means creating more stress and anxiety —and it's just not worth it. Until you let it go, you can't fill your bank account. In order to do so, you're going to have to give up some control. You cannot do it all.

Don't be fooled. The ego mindset isn't just about thinking you're the only person that can run the business. It also comes in the form of stories you tell yourself.

"I'm bad with technology."

"I hate Facebook and Instagram."

"I'm not a good writer."

"I'm scared of making videos."

"I'm lazy and inconsistent."

To a certain extent, all of this self-talk keeps you safe. Your ego is there to safeguard your current reality. Every time you're hit with the possibility of leveling up or changing where you are today, your ego steps in, whether in the form of fear or just discomfort.

The reason your brain does this is that it hasn't caught up yet to the fact that you're not a caveman being chased by an apex predator. Adaptation is a slow process, and your brain is constantly wired for fear. What your brain knows will keep you safe, it will encourage you to repeat. It's up to you to choose the scary thing anyway.

Ego also leads to mixing and matching strategies—a recipe for failure. A process like the one I'm teaching you in this book works when applied consistently and in its entirety. When you think you're smart enough, clever enough, or experienced enough to ignore what's being taught and instead do it your own way, you're letting your ego take the lead.

If you knew better, you'd be doing better. Don't let your ego sabotage your success.

Perfectionism

Confidence is the reward, not the requirement.

So many people spend time thinking and planning but never taking action. They want everything to be perfect before they implement anything—but implementation is what gives you the confidence you're looking for.

Waiting for something to be "ready" is just your brain's way of protecting you from failure, disappointment, and risk—but those things are unavoidable. No one is ever fully ready for change. We have to make peace with that fact and get comfortable with the concept of launching and learning.

You don't get to be great without failure—without launching, learning, and then iterating. Business is all about problem solving. If you're constantly waiting for the perfect answer, you never get to learn what the *right* solution is. If you go about everything in your business (and your life) from a place of fear of failure, nothing will ever happen to or for you, good or bad.

Lack of Clarity

You need a clear vision of what it is you're working toward, or you'll end up with a business you didn't want. It's that simple. You'll get stuck trying to figure out how to get to the business you want, day after day, with no real roadmap to get there.

I was guilty of this in my early days. I was always working to get the next deal done, and then the next deal, and then the deal after that, without any intentionality or clarity in terms of what I actually wanted my life to look like.

Too many agents, when asked about their goals, will say something like, "I want to double my business." But when asked how, they have no idea. They'll go through goal-setting exercises (often recommended by their brokerage) every single quarter, and yet the next year, they find themselves at the exact same place they started. Often, it's because they did nothing to change their trajectory for one of two reasons: They lacked clarity about how to reach their goals, or their goals were too vague to be achievable.

The approach to take instead is to ask yourself what you want. What does your perfect day look like? What does it look like five years from now? How do you work backwards to create a business that's going to create that perfect day?

Going through the motions versus having a plan is like the difference between accuracy and precision. Accuracy gets you in the neighborhood. Precision puts you in the house.

Insecurity

Beyoncé gets nervous. Yes, even Beyoncé.

At the end of the day, we're all facing challenges and opportunities in our life from a similar human experience. Incredibly successful people still get nervous. They stress about their taxes. They still make mistakes. They screw things up. They fail.

If you let your impostor syndrome stand in your way of moving forward and making real change—well, for a potential client, the choice is going to be either you or someone else.

Who will you let it be?

Shiny Object Syndrome

Redesigning your website, launching a podcast, creating a YouTube show—if any of these things aren't directly contributing to solving the number-one problem in your business, then you're procrastinating. You're simply chasing the next shiny object.

This is just another form of procrastination, another protection mechanism, because you're afraid to focus on one thing and fail at it. Going all-in on one thing feels a lot scarier than giving small fragments of your attention to many things. So you try a million essentially unrelated projects. When they don't work, you reinforce that negative-feedback loop. You know you can fail and get back up, which is more familiar than success.

And by now, you know where following familiar thoughts gets you.

PUT YOURSELF FIRST

Setting an intention every day can be a powerful habit.

When I was still selling real estate and having a lot of anxiety, I started journaling every day. Every morning, before I ever looked at my phone, I sat down and wrote. Before that, I was the typical agent who woke up every morning, rolled over, and immediately started checking my emails.

I set the intention that I was going to take care of myself *first*. I had to set boundaries, particularly when it came to my phone. I'm willing to bet you're nodding your head yet again right now because you *know* you need to do the same.

Once I started with that habit, I took the idea even further—and the change that resulted was massive. I set a rule for myself that my phone stayed on "do not disturb" until I had taken care of three things—my body, mind, and spirit. That meant I had to work out, journal, and either listen to a podcast or read a chapter or two of a book. Once those three things were done, the world got access to me because I'd taken care of me first.

Now, not everyone's morning routine has to look like mine, but I do believe that you need to adopt some process that gets you in the right headspace, the right mindset, to start your day. Because, let's face it, we live in a world where people are constantly pulling at you. This is especially true in real estate. Everybody wants something from you, whether it's your team, your family, or your clients. This also doesn't have to mean that you're getting up at 5am and doing a three-hour routine. Make what you do work for your life.

If instead you start every day answering calls for your attention, you'll feel very empty very quickly.

Millionaire Mindset

Anyone who has built a seven-figure real estate business understands that there are three things they have to protect and leverage no matter what:

- Time

- Money

- Energy

People with a millionaire mindset know that they have to leverage the money they have by investing or spending it sensibly. However, most people tend to think about money from a scarcity mindset. They think they have to hoard their money or spend it on things that are lifestyle-based.

You have to be less attached to your money, and being less attached takes discipline. If you're going to be incredibly successful in something like real estate, you have to tell yourself that money can always be made again.

Most of the money being exchanged daily does not exist in a vault somewhere in the form of either paper or gold. The numbers in your account are just an idea. It's as easy to see a low number as it is a high one.

What you can't make more of is time.

Successful people leverage time whenever they can. This was a concept I struggled with in my early days. The idea here is that you make yourself more efficient and delegate tasks often. That means having the right team instead of a big team, one to whom you can delegate outcomes, not just tasks (a pillar we'll visit later in the book). When you have the right team in place, you empower them to produce outcomes. It's critical that you cut down on the time dedicated to tasks outside of your expertise.

As important as it is to leverage time and money, energy may be the most important of the three. It takes more energy to do things that are not in your "Kinetic Domain." I'll talk more about this in a later chapter.

The short version is this: If you had to sit down and do a task you aren't good at (for example, accounting) all day long, you'd hate every minute of it. You'd probably feel physically exhausted after an hour, if you made it that far. Conversely, when you do a task to which you're well suited, you feel energized and lose yourself in it. You'll also do it more efficiently and at a higher level than others will because you genuinely like it. There are people who feel energized by spreadsheets. I'm definitely not one of them.

Be smart with your energy. What often ends up happening is that managing energy and time become intertwined—and they shouldn't. You can spend a great deal of time working on something and feel more energized afterward, but you don't want to lose track of being efficient with your time, even when doing the things that keep you energized.

People who are less successful trade time for money, or they prioritize money over time and energy. They'll tell themselves they could hire somebody to perform a specific task for $15 an hour, but because they live with a scarcity mindset, they decide to do it themselves. That leaves them with less time and less energy because it's a task they'd rather not do. Once again, they become the bottleneck in their business because they're spending too much time on non-income-generating activities.

The difference between someone who has a business and someone who has a seven-figure business is this:

If you *are* the business, then you don't *have* a business.

If you build a real estate business that is entirely dependent on you, your time, and your energy, you will eventually get to a point where you won't be able to scale and you can't grow. The worst part of all of that is you'll end up hating what you once loved.

Values, Mission, and Vision

We hear all the time that the market needs to know your brand's value, mission, and vision—and those things *are* important. But I want to help you look at them in a different way.

Without establishing your core values and mission, and without a clear vision, you will essentially run your business based on what you are feeling on a given day. This happens a lot, particularly when it comes to marketing, and it's a mistake. Agents post on their social media based on the mood they're in rather than keeping their messaging aligned with their values, mission, and vision.

Also, when everything in your business is based on you rather than values, mission, and vision, your team will end up hating you. Harsh, but true. It is essential that the people in your organization or on your team understand your core values, mission, and vision.

This ties back to the notion of clarity. Your brand should have its own set of values, mission and vision, with the understanding that your brand or your business is a separate entity from you. Said another way, your brand or your business does not have to share your *personal* values, mission, and vision.

Imagine being part of a business whose mission pivots at the whim of its owner. They go on some vacation that changes their entire perspective on life, and now they decide they're going to run their organization based on these new principles they've adopted. The entire team would be forced to stop, change direction, and rebuild. It would drive you insane, and likely out of the company altogether.

When you separate your brand's values, mission, and vision from your own, you're free to change your personal vision without harming your brand's progress. It's a win-win. The idea might seem trivial, but people don't just randomly choose an agent. They often make their decision based on your brand's *why*. Your clients, audience, and team will all gather behind your brand when you have a strong why.

Now, if you've come from one of the larger national brokerages, you've likely heard the concept of your "why" thrown around a lot. You're taught that your "why" should be external—and that can be okay, but I also strongly feel that there's an element of martyrdom involved when we choose our whys in this manner.

It's okay for your why to be a better life, or for something even bigger than you personally. For example, my why is that I want to transform the real estate industry, and my personal life is a part of that. But I also have selfish things in my why, too. I want to live a certain lifestyle. I want to be able to provide certain things for my family. I want to be able to travel with my husband.

But those whys are not my team's whys. Just like our core values and mission aren't my team's personal core values or vision for their lives. But our core values set the expectation of how we show up in the business every day, how we solve problems, and how we set and meet goals. Everyone who works in or on the business knows the business' why, and it serves as a lens through which all decisions are filtered.

Your personal why should be something that's going to get you up and out of bed every day. It's important for you to have a personal stake in your own why. It should not be something you feel like you have to choose because it's expected of you. Give yourself permission to have your personal why be just that—personal. Just as you can rely on motivation every day, your why can't only be for other people.

Focus Versus Opportunity

The average real estate agent receives income from seven different sources outside of real estate.[2] Seven!

---

[2] https://www.linkedin.com/pulse/7-income-streams-most-millionaires-manoj-arora

How can you focus on being the best in the industry when you're working six other side hustles?

If you don't, at this moment, have a seven-figure real estate business that operates like a machine—and if you're reading this book, you probably don't—then it is *way* too early to start another business.

Here's what happens: You start to get momentum in your real estate business, and it feels good. You finally know what you're doing. Your confidence goes up, you have some money to spare. Suddenly, there are opportunities everywhere. Everyone has a business idea. Everybody wants you to invest in something. You put on your super-optimistic pants and ask yourself, "How hard could it be?"

Then you spend a little bit of time on the new venture—a few days here, a few days there—and before you know it, you realize you're not actually focusing on any one business. Instead, you've split your time and resources before you had them available to split. A bit more time passes, and the new business takes up even more of your time; your real estate business begins to suffer as a result.

This is called the Dunning-Kruger Effect.[3] Your confidence is high, but your competence is low. Too many agents move on to the next thing before becoming truly competent—as agents, as

---

[3] https://thedecisionlab.com/biases/dunning-kruger-effect

leaders, as visionaries. You have to focus on your main real estate business until you have established a finely tuned machine. Focus has a compound effect, and you need all of that focus in *one* area to cash out on that effect.

When you convince yourself that you can do more than what's possible, you end up losing not only your focus, but also leverage, and ultimately money. If you have to hustle to make a new opportunity work, the chances of it working alongside your real estate business are very low, if not non-existent.

Risk

As a real estate agent, you come up against risk every day. But nobody likes risk. And, because of that, people end up ignoring it instead of confronting and managing it.

There are four types of risk.

First, there is unavoidable risk. By that I don't mean that you have no choice in the risk, but that it's the risk and cost of having a business; and it has to be monitored.

Then there's avoidable risk. With this variety of risk, you can make choices to avoid a certain outcome. For example, you decide you won't spend X number of dollars on Facebook ads until you know the outcome of that expenditure.

Next, there's variable risk. This is the risk you choose to take on and can do something about. For example, if your month is ending up as budgeted, you can produce revenue by sending out an investment opportunity to your current database. There's only a small amount of risk involved here. This would be the small risk of "unsubscribes" and having people not "like" this opportunity.

Lastly, there's transferable risk, which is risk you can pay to have mediated with insurance.

Successful agents manage each one of these types of risk on a daily basis. They understand that momentum in the real estate business is based on reducing the right amount of friction or risk while maintaining a high enough volume of it to be rewarded.

Most people with normal day jobs see being a real estate agent as high risk, and they believe that agents have a high-risk tolerance. I actually believe the opposite is true for the most successful agents. They see the world as high risk and mitigate that risk by taking control of it.

Fear of Failure—and Success

There was a single weekend in which I did more deals than I had the entire year before.

I didn't understand how to process what had just happened. A massive up-leveling had just occurred—and it scared me.

We hear so much about the fear of failure, but so few actually talk about the fear of success.

Failure is a data point. It tells us exactly where we went wrong. It tells us which part of a plan or strategy didn't go the way we thought it would. Success, on the other hand, is actually far more terrifying because, more often than not, we're not 100 percent sure how we got there. We have a hard time identifying the one thing that actually made all of these good things happen.

Our brains are better wired for failure than they are for success. As animals, our biology has evolved to protect us in such a way that success can feel like failure. Think about it—most of us can clearly imagine huge, catastrophic failures. We can predict the scenario and imagine what it looks and feels like. But when we come in contact with success for the first time, it lets us access our ego or pride in a way we've never done before.

This is why so many agents who find early success lose it. They don't know how to react to their newfound success and freedom. Their egos inflate, and they start to believe they're invincible. Then they start making emotional decisions, which turn into bad choices. It's the same reason many people ignore their debt and pretend it's not real. It's also why so many people who are successful get out of control, overstating their success to themselves.

Both failure and success build character—but you need to be able to attach the process to the result. You have to pinpoint why you succeeded or why you failed. That's where character is built.

Consider that nothing is forever. It doesn't matter if you're successful right now—you might not be tomorrow.

If you consider yourself a failure, you still have value and the opportunity to use your gifts and strengths in any situation.

NO MORE "LONE WOLF"

When I handed that phone to Yves in tears, I knew I needed help. It didn't matter anymore if the business was serving my ego, allowing me to go on thinking I could do everything. I had to be honest with myself—I could no longer be the only person answering the phone.

Now, this might seem a natural segue into building your team—but not so fast. Before we do that, we need to talk about your clients and your Signature System.

Chapter Four

PILLAR THREE: CLIENTS AND THE SIGNATURE SYSTEM

I've seen many agents build a name for themselves purely on the claim that they perform some sort of magic. This sounds great, but if you don't standardize your process, it can become a big problem if you ever want to be able to scale.

I know this because I was guilty of it, too.

I built a business where everyone knew *my* name. It was all about me. Referrals were coming in fast and furious—but the clients only wanted to speak to me directly. They didn't even want to talk to my assistant. They wanted to know when *I* would be calling them. Because of this, everything became single-threaded through me—every conversation, every email, every phone call.

My mistake was that I didn't have a repeatable system.

The general public believes that most agents are making things up as we go, flying by the seat of our pants. That's not entirely untrue for most agents, and some even do this freestyling thing really well. But when clients start believing an agent is the only one who can help them, and the agent positions themselves that way in their marketing, they find themselves in a situation where they've built a great reputation, but they have no repeatable system or intellectual property. And that's not scalable.

Just as in the last chapter, there is an ego component to this. It feels good to be in demand, to feel like everybody wants you. The ego account gets filled up very quickly with this kind of thinking. But once again, if you think you're special and that no one else can do what you do—and maybe even that members of your team can't do it as well as you do—you'll become the bottleneck. Your bandwidth, energy, and time will be the ceiling that prevents your business from growing any further.

The time component is especially important here. If everyone believes you're special, you'll find yourself with a whole group of clients—or a whole group of agents on your team—who feel entitled to your time. When that happens, there's no trust in your *business*. There's only trust in *you*.

If we're thinking about this in terms of a seven-figure model, it's practically impossible for you to hit those kinds of numbers if you're doing the $10 per hour tasks, making and taking every phone call, and looking at every piece of paperwork. Even if you have an assistant, you'll become the ceiling of your business because you can work with only so many clients and there are only so many hours in a day.

All that said, it's totally understandable why I made this mistake, and so many other agents continue to make it. Doing everything yourself serves you when you're small and just starting out. However, when it comes to setting up your business, this kind of short-term thinking leads to long-term pain.

DEVELOP A SIGNATURE SYSTEM

You can't collaborate with clients or pass them off to anyone else on your team if you don't have a Signature System—a standardized client process that is name branded and marketed.

A Signature System solves the problem of clients who refuse to work with anyone other than you. It will give you a much easier time sharing your leads and clients among the people on your team because your clients have bought into the system—not just you. Using that system, you can build out all of your standard operating procedures. This means that your team has the ability to execute your system at a very high level—no babysitting necessary. Every single client is taken care of, maybe even better than you could have taken care of them on your own.

Clarity is Key

When developing your system, it's important that you keep it simple. You want to structure it so that clients understand it right away. Tell them what the system is and why they need it. What are they getting? What is it that you actually do? It doesn't matter who comes through your door or whose door you go through, you're focusing on the same basic areas to create results. All of this should be geared toward creating results for your clients and giving them the best experience possible.

Remember when we discussed the avatar for your ideal client? Now is the time to look at the things your ideal client needs to have in order for them to see the results they want. What's going to make them happy? What problems are they facing? You will build your solution based on that answer.

Make Your Own Pillars

You want your system to have a methodology in the same way this book has a methodology. Once you have the pillars, or cornerstones, of your methodology fully built out, they become the foundation for your system or process.

Name the entire system—and each pillar—so that it becomes the core of your work and the backbone of your business. This system will be what sets you apart from the crowd. It also gives you the framework you'll use to build out *all* of your services.

Your client has to understand why each step happens at that particular part of the process. Explain the pillar and what it entails but limit that explanation to just a few sentences. Boil your system down to its absolute essence for your clients. If you tend to get wordy when describing things—don't. Your descriptions must be refined and clear.

Get Them from A to B

If you're reading this book, you probably already have a process of some sort, though you likely haven't nailed it down, documented it, or named it. The fact that you haven't done this contributes to the perception that you're flying by the seat of your pants or that no one else can "do it" other than you.

It's important to figure out what you're actually doing because your Signature System will become your unique value proposition. It's your differentiator. The most important thing you will express through your system description is how you're going to help your clients get from A to B—from their current situation to their desired outcome.

People don't move because it's fun. It's not. People move to solve life problems or to build a better future. So, the key here is to understand what *isn't* serving your potential clients in their current situation and to understand what they see as the vision of their future after the move.

To convey this, you should have a guide that walks them through the process. This same guide should also serve as your listing conversation documentation (more on this in the next chapter).

The System as Marketing

Your Signature System serves in a dual role, as both marketing content and assets. You can use your system to reiterate the different steps of your process, why you do them that way, and case studies where you've used your system effectively. This is literally what you are selling to the client.

You can—and should—use your Signature System as a cornerstone of your marketing. It can serve as an education piece so that people buy into not just you, but what you do. The system becomes a secondary piece to make your business scalable. It makes the handoff of things within the process so much easier.

If you've laid out your system in clear terms, addressed your clients' pains, and offered solutions, you'll have their buy-in. If you've done your job correctly, this buy-in eliminates objections when you explain that you'll be bringing in another member of your team who specializes in solving a particular part of their problem.

The creation of the Signature System can seem overwhelming, but it definitely doesn't need to be—not if you follow the method below.

The first thing you want to do is to start with the buyer's pains and problems. What are they in their most specific form? It's important that you don't just guess but that you find out from clients—past or present. For example, an upsizer might realize that the cute starter home they bought isn't actually a family friend when they're lugging their child up and down a staircase to change them several times a day.

You want five steps *maximum* in your process and only want to include the steps that your client or prospect will see. Ask yourself:

"How can I take what I would normally do and apply this very specifically to solve the main problems that I've identified?"

For the upsizers, most agents will start with a needs and wants assessment. I disagree with starting there because upsizers often aren't looking at the bigger picture. They need help seeing that their current home can serve larger wealth-building goals. They need help creating a long-term plan and ensuring that the move they're about to make sets them up for success. What you would do for someone selling their third home is very different than for someone selling their first.

Knowing and acting on this is how you build lifelong clients. Remember: You're not just working for the transaction. Your goal is to create influence with that person—for life. You want to be their trusted advisor forever—and becoming that advisor starts with the first step of this process.

Every step has to be very intentional. Ask yourself why the next step you choose is important and why it's in that order. When you do this, you're able to look at a whole process holistically and break it down into steps for your clients to understand.

Your relationships and trusted sources can also be included in this process, too. Your "team," including your mortgage lender, lawyers, etc., can be very useful in helping take some initial stress off the clients' minds.

Automation in the process is great and necessary, but keep in mind that your clients never want anything to *feel* automated. They want to feel that their relationship with you is special.

At the end of the day, everyone just wants to feel seen and heard. When you can do that for your clients, they'll never want to go anywhere else. And it changes the types of conversations that leads have with you. Every day, our members get emails asking, "Do you have space in your schedule to take on new clients?" and not "I'm interviewing five other agents. Can you do a deal for 1 percent?"

When you sound like a professional with a solution that caters to people's problems, you become the go-to expert in their eyes. And that means your sales conversation isn't really about sales as much as it is about confirming the fact that *you* want to work with *them*.

Chapter Five

PILLAR FOUR:
SALES CONVERSATIONS

I was in my early twenties when I entered the real estate profession under the banner of a major brokerage, one of the big players. I'd gone through all of their trainings, including their framework for the listing presentation.

They essentially taught us how to talk *at* clients. They coached us to present as though we were giving a speech to a room full of people. We went in so cold that we had to educate the client about the entire market and process while also trying to get the person to trust us and build rapport.

I distinctly remember one client presentation in particular. I was young, nervous, and sitting in a million-dollar home. While the wife seemed mildly interested in my presentation, she was far from engaged; her husband repeatedly picked up his Blackberry as I spoke. It was clear I was losing them both. I had a moment when I realized that none of what I was doing felt right. I was standing as I gave the presentation; in other words, I wasn't even physically meeting them at their level. I realized in that moment that I needed to forget everything I'd been taught and do what felt right.

I took a deep breath—and then I sat on the sofa with them.

I started asking them personal questions about the home. Why did they buy their house in the first place? What were the things they loved most about it? What was motivating them to sell it now?

The entire feel of the discussion shifted. They started telling me stories about things they'd experienced while living there. They were engaged. They were talking *to* me, and I was talking *to* them— we were having an actual conversation. In doing so, I was still able to weave into my "presentation" all of the information I wanted to, but now they were actually hearing me because we were having a conversation. I wasn't just talking *at* them.

The listing presentation as you probably know it today is yet another form of old-school selling. Much like a door-to-door salesman, you probably feel like you have to get your pitch in before a potential client slams the door in your face.

Your relationship with your clients is not a corporate one. And so, it only makes sense that the tone of listing presentations—or, rather, *conversations*—has to change. The choice to buy or sell a home is grounded in emotion. If you don't tap into that emotion, you're probably going to lose out to another agent. If you base the conversations *only* on numbers (listing price, commission percentage, etc.), you're not truly building value.

Your value to the customer is also not in how much you are willing to do. You answer your phone 24/7? Good for you—that's not value. If your systems and services are set up properly, you shouldn't have to do that. Your clients shouldn't have questions for you at two o'clock in the morning. They don't have to chase you for anything because they already have what they need from your system. *That* is value.

Here's the thing—as is the case with so many other elements of the business, agents haven't been taught how to have these conversations in an effective or resonant way. No one taught you what demonstrating your value or service should *actually* look like. Instead, you've been taught to compete for business in the same way every other agent always has, and it's getting you nowhere.

THE DESTINATION—NOT THE AIRPLANE

After that moment with the couple, I began studying sales from other industries to see if I could apply their methods to real estate.

In the process, I discovered that way too many agents feel like they should be selling themselves.

When you go to a travel agent, they don't tell you about how they're going to stick you in an aluminum tube, throw you through the sky, invite you to share a bathroom with three hundred strangers, and feed you terrible food. That's not what people want to hear about!

Travel agents sell the *destination*—that resort in Mexico on the front of the brochure—*not* the airplane.

But so many agents are selling the airplane.

Those agents go into a listing presentation focused on the selling process when all potential clients really want to know is whether or not you can get them where they want to go. They want to know that you understand them, that you are capable of selling their property, and that they won't have to worry once they sign with you.

Set Expectations

The first thing to do when you have any kind of sales conversation is set expectations. Even though you are having a conversation, your clients need an agenda, so they understand what to expect. They need and want you to hold their hand and walk them through the process. When you set expectations, it allows you to direct the flow of the conversation.

Ask More Questions

The most successful salespeople ask an average of seventy-two questions per conversation. Now, you might not ask *that* many questions, but your goal should be to ask as many questions of the client as you can. The deeper you dig, the more real the conversation will be and the more connected to you the potential clients will feel.

Whenever you're in a sales conversation, you want to go seven layers deeper. Think about it like dip. Sure, the cheese on top is great. But if you really want to get to the good stuff, you've got to put in the effort to get that chip deep into each of those delicious layers. Treat sales conversations like an amazing dip.

The things clients tell you at the beginning of the conversation will be surface level and essentially useless. That's why one of the most effective and frequent questions you should be asking in your conversations with clients is "Can you tell me more?"

Listen Without an Agenda

Let the client speak more than you do.

Most real estate agents feel like they should be doing most of the talking. Wrong.

As a general rule of thumb, your client should be talking two-thirds of the time in a listing conversation. Repeat their wants and needs back to them in your own words. Confirm that what you're hearing is accurate. This will let your clients know you've understood them.

Treat Your Clients Like a Friend

Don't use big industry words. Speak in layman's terms. Don't try to sound smart. Don't try too hard or act overly professional. I know that some agents want to be viewed like a doctor or a lawyer. But remember—you're *not* a doctor or a lawyer. Real estate is an extremely personal profession, and each situation should be viewed this way.

Of course, you don't want to go too far in the other direction, either. Don't offer too much personal information about yourself. That said, if you have been in a situation similar to the one your client is in, don't be afraid to share that anecdote as a way of relating.

Even better is talking about a previous client in a similar circumstance who you were able to help. This will inspire confidence in you and your abilities. People want to know that there's a light at the end of the tunnel. Your client can't see it from where they are. Your job is to help them get there.

Get on the Same Side of the Table

Never badmouth anyone.

If your client has had a bad experience before, empathize but don't commiserate. A lot of people have been in terrible situations with other agents, and sadly, many agents capitalize on that information. Not only will they trash-talk other agents in the conversation, but they'll also take to social media and share that bad experience to make themselves look better. All that does is make the whole industry look bad.

Acknowledge your client's experience—then share how your Signature System ensures that they won't have that experience with you.

Resist Over-explaining and Overselling

Find out what your client's top objectives are. There are usually two or three.

Then, go deep on aligning your services to those top objectives. You can offer samples of what else you can do in your Signature System, but if you go through every tiny little detail, you'll end up giving a standard listing presentation. Trust that the client will ask questions about anything else they need answers to after you've given them an overview of what you do and why you do it.

Don't make assumptions. This goes back to asking questions. The more you ask, the more information you have and the more you can tailor your services to what the client *actually* wants and needs.

Handle Objections Before They Occur

You *have* to know what the most common objections are when you go into any sales conversation. Once you've got twenty or so listing conversations under your belt, you'll know in advance what those objections are and how to deal with them.

If you sense a financial concern, don't shy away from it. Agents tend to ignore situations that make either us or the client uncomfortable. Don't do that. Instead, dive into any point where you notice the client hesitating. When you're trying to build that trust, it is always better to address something proactively than reactively—because those objections that were there from the beginning will always come up again at the end.

For example, one especially common objection that comes up when dealing with younger clients is that they need to review everything with their parents. To handle that, ensure that all decision makers will be present when you book the listing appointment. This is *always* going to be better because you can build relationships with *everyone*. The last thing you want is a younger client trying to relay what you said and not doing it justice.

Once you've overcome the objection, you also have to come to a mutual understanding that the objection is no longer a concern. Get verification from the client that you're now on the same page. If you don't get that verification, continue to address the objection until you do.

There are five steps to handling objections well.

Acknowledge

People expect resistance to an objection. Give your clients the opposite with phrases like "Of course" or "I totally understand."

Accept

When you accept your client's objection as their truth, you validate them and build trust. Again, put yourself on the same side of the table.

Shut Up

Once you've handled the objection, stop talking. Get it in your head that the first person who speaks loses. Don't oversell your response.

Pinpoint the Pain Point

Go back to the reason the client sought you out. Why is it important for them to sell their home at this particular time?

Close

You have to be comfortable asking for the close. If you don't ask for it, you'll likely go in circles. Give your client the opening to say "yes" by asking them directly if they are ready. Be confident enough to ask and it will raise their confidence in you.

You don't always have to go for the hard close. Make the close feel more like an invitation. The way you go about this is entirely dependent on the client's demeanor. Sometimes it can be as simple as:

"Do you have any other questions? Are you ready?"

"Is there anything else we need to cover before we sign this paperwork?"

Of course, there are also situations in which clients are legitimately scared and will interview fifty agents and still never make a decision because they don't trust themselves. In that situation, you might say something like:

"It seems like there's a trust issue here. It's either that you don't trust me or that you don't trust yourself to make the right decision. Do you know which one it is?"

That might sound bolder than you're comfortable with, but the key to good sales is to say the thing that others don't want to say or that your client might not even be aware of.

70 Percent Versus 30 Percent

The whole purpose of handling objections is to figure out which camp a client is in. We can break this into a 70/30 split. 70 percent of objections are a trust objection. The other 30 percent are based on a legitimate concern. The 70 percent is the hardest part to manage because a trust objection can be a difficult obstacle to overcome.

The best way to handle the 70 percent zone is with case studies demonstrating how you have helped clients in situations similar to theirs, along with building rapport by asking as many questions as you can.

The more understood and emotionally connected your client feels to you, the better. It pays to have a case study in the back of your mind for every objection you can think of. They can help you build trust through legitimacy without having to boast that you're number one or that you've worked with X amount of people. Clients don't connect with that.

You cannot be afraid to address what kind of an objection you're getting. Instead of letting the elephant remain in the room to do cartwheels, call it out as quickly as you can. When you're able to say that you understand that there's some trust that needs to be built here, you can not only acknowledge the elephant, but escort it out. Then you can ask them what they need to feel more comfortable. Sometimes the solution might just be connecting them to a past client to speak with.

Empathy

Many agents get so wrapped in doing deals that they forget how much moving sucks. As I have mentioned previously, the only reason people move is because their current situation isn't serving them anymore. They have a destination in mind and a desired situation. They want to believe that getting there through this awful process is going to be worth it.

Now, you might be thinking that you're not the touchy-feely type. You just want to get your deals done. You're good with the hustle and grind and aren't concerned with making a connection with your clients.

That's fine—but understand that people make decisions emotionally. People apply logic to their emotions to help them sleep at night. It's why a client can fall in love with a home that should be totally wrong for them. Emotions override logic.

If you're operating with a hustle-and-grind mentality, your clients are going to feel sold to. They're going to see you as the car salesman, and you're not going to win as often.

This mentality likely isn't your fault. You've been sold scripts by your brokerage and, at this point, probably don't trust yourself to have an actual conversation with your clients. You have been trained to ignore what probably got you into real estate in the first place—the fact that you're good with people. The scripts suppress your natural instincts to have an organic conversation with your clients.

Once you return to that, you'll be better than any prescribed talking points you've been given.

The real estate industry is becoming more and more competitive and advanced. There are more disruptors that are going to push out the people who use scripts and keep their license to do two deals a year.

If you want to thrive, you have to do better. You're not just selling the house. You're selling the whole emotional experience. You're selling the trust clients need. For most people, buying or selling a home is the biggest investment of their lives.

THEY SIGNED WITH ME

Back to the clients I told you about at the beginning of this chapter.

I was the third person that the couple had interviewed that day. I was also the youngest and the least experienced.

However…

At the end of our conversation, after I had shifted gears, the clients told me that I was the only agent who really talked to them. I was the only one who asked what they wanted and needed. They felt like I cared.

And because of that, they decided to go with me.

It's worth pointing out that I was a long shot for this listing because of the caliber of agents I was up against. The others were big names in the area. But the couple told me that those agents walked into the room acting as if it was a done deal. They assumed they were going to get the listing.

That's not to say that you shouldn't be confident in your skills. But, again, make sure your ego account isn't running the show because your bank account is what will end up suffering. Because my spur-of-the-moment approach was more organic, the couple felt more involved in the decision. Going off script was key to tapping into the emotion behind their decision not only to list with me, but in all of the decisions they subsequently made in the process of selling their home.

Not only that, but our initial conversation helped them to see me as their guide because it focused on where they wanted to be and showed them how I would help them get there.

You need to strive for these organic discussions in your listing conversations, but remember—they can't just be about you, the one-person show. Every single person on your (eventual) team has to have their own way of conducting these conversations. While everyone needs to be well-versed in your Signature System, they'll have to have their own signature way of having the conversation. Otherwise, you're giving them a script.

We're that much closer to talking about how you will build that team and lead them—but first we need to get clear on the operations of your business.

Chapter Six

PILLAR FIVE: OPERATIONS

When agents get their mindset, their marketing, their Signature System, and their sales conversations in place, things really start humming. Leads and referrals come in left and right, and these agents are busier than they have ever been. They realize they can't do it all themselves or they will end up where I did—burned out.

It's good when agents have this realization—but it often leads to a big mistake: outsourcing or hiring for a job before you actually know how to do that job well.

As a new agent, my brokerage brought me up in the model that once you get to a certain level of business, the first thing you do is hire an assistant. When I was getting to that stage of my business,

I thought that model didn't make sense. If I could automate my marketing, there had to be other parts of my business I could automate through technology as well. It was around this time that I began reading Tim Ferriss and his concept of "eliminate, automate, outsource." Notice that outsourcing is the last option and not the first.

But I didn't do it that way. I looked around me, and nobody else was doing it that way. So I chose the safe option. Remember how I mentioned that this leads to nothing good? Well…I hired an assistant, grew my team, and did it all without automation and or proper systems in place. It ended up being very expensive and wasteful.

Admittedly, one of the reasons I did it that way was because the technology I needed didn't exist at the time, so I fell back on what I had been taught. I didn't have anything that could connect the different accounts I had without complex coding; I didn't have things that created the kinds of communication automations that would trigger next steps.

So I hired an administrative assistant.

Without going into detail, the assistant wasn't a good fit, and we ended up parting ways rather quickly, even though she'd come highly recommended by my broker. That was my first expensive lesson.

The problem wasn't just her. Yes, she oversold her skill set, but I also didn't have the systems in place to set her up for success.

There are a lot of agents who will tell you the same story—that they hired an admin who was terrible. But that happens when agents create a giant mess and then expect someone who makes far less money than they do to be able to clean up that mess. Hiring someone and saying, "Fix this disorganized chaos in a month, or I'll fire you" won't cut it; it's not reasonable or fair.

Without a solid operational system, you are setting yourself up for disappointment and setting your assistant up for failure. You need to have certain systems and processes sorted out *before* you bring that admin in. You need a proper onboarding procedure and system they can be plugged into.

AGENTS DON'T UNDERSTAND SYSTEMS

Sorry, but it's true. I told you at the start of this book that I was not going to sugarcoat things. Agents all want and covet systems, but they don't really understand what a system *is*. It's an organized framework or method that produces a specific result.

For example, a Pre-Listing Staging System is a series of steps that are carried out in the same order, with tasks and outcomes delegated to the same people who will produce comparable results, listing to listing. The system likely designates specific people to perform key jobs, and software and tools to communicate and manage the project, as well as a budget and a clear completion point.

Sometimes, you will need a system within a system. For instance, many of our members have team members who deal with transaction management while others deal with marketing collateral for a listing. Those two sub-teams have their own systems and procedures for getting to that completion point. They also have a project manager with a system and procedure for making sure that no balls are dropped on the bigger goal of getting a listing to go live.

The important thing to remember is that not everything will be built to perfection. The first version of your system is a starting point, not the end goal. It will change many times. As new people join your team, they will find better, more streamlined ways of doing things. These will all be incorporated into new versions of the system.

ENERGY AUDIT

Of course your systems help your business run efficiently; your Operations team ensures that the *systems* also run efficiently. To see what systems you need, look at your business from all angles. For every single person on your team, for every process, you want every process and every single person on your team to operate like a finely tuned machine. Once you achieve that, you'll end up with the freedom you desire.

Every entrepreneur, no matter what industry, has a big vision and is prepared to solve problems for a living. The thing about solving problems is that every time you solve one, more problems arise. It's incredibly important that you're okay with the fact that even when your business becomes that finely tuned machine, like even the most high-performing car, you'll need to perform maintenance to keep it running smoothly.

The first step in building that smooth-running machine is performing what I call an Energy Audit.

Energy isn't bound by time. People can spend a lot of time and energy on things they love, and it doesn't drain them. Happy people who love their business are people who maximize their energy. You need to change your relationship with your work and how you operate within your business. There are far too many agents spending too much time doing things they hate to do. When that happens, everyone in your life suffers. Your business suffers. Your clients suffer. No one is getting your best.

That is what happened to me.

You want to elevate your energy so that you can have the biggest possible impact on your community, your family, and your business. You can do this by auditing your energy and organizing the tasks in your business into what I call the four different "domains of energy."

Gravitational Energy Domain

You're likely good at many things, great at a more limited number, truly an expert in only a few areas; this is true for everyone. Also like everyone, you have areas and tasks you're inept at and don't like doing. But chances are, you're spending a lot of time on them, they weigh you down like gravity, demoralize you, and keep you from unlimited upward mobility.

You should not engage in these "Gravitational Domain" tasks. They vary by person, but often they include administrative work—paperwork, financials—the tiny details on the backend of things. My Gravitational Domain includes things like bookkeeping, which I hate and am bad at.

If the thought of being inept at things or not having access to everything makes you feel uncomfortable, your ego account is cashing checks. It's okay for people on your team to be better than you at things. That is just a part of growth. Embrace it. There's a reason that Jeff Bezos doesn't pack boxes in an Amazon warehouse.

Inertial Energy Domain

Almost worse than not being good at something and not liking it is being good at something that you hate doing. Again, everybody has these. I can create a spreadsheet if I really have to, but I despise creating them. On the other hand, my COO's eyes light up when she gets to create a new resource to keep the team organized.

The tasks you're doing to keep the business going but not growing are in the "Inertial Domain." If you think back to high-school science, inertia is the tendency of objects in motion to stay in motion at the same speed unless an outside force acts on them.

The reason you're inefficient at these tasks is that human brains are wired naturally to steer us away from pain. It's the same impulse that lets you know if you've accidentally put your hand on a hot burner. Our brains don't like us to do things that make us physically, mentally, or emotionally uncomfortable for longer than is absolutely necessary. When we do, they will always try to distract us.

And usually, they succeed. This is when shiny objects look their shiniest. Instead of working on the design of that new marketing asset, you might spend a half hour looking up how to start a podcast or YouTube channel instead.

The problem is that when you guiltily come back to that design tool, your brain is no longer focused on that task, and it takes time to get back into the design groove. An outside force—be it the internet, your phone, or even this book if you picked it up as a distraction—has negatively impacted your brain's ability to focus. This is a phenomenon known as context switching. Every time you context switch, you lose valuable minutes in your day.

The things you're bad at and don't like doing will actually keep you focused because they require your full attention to be even minimally competent at them. Because you're good at the tasks in your Inertial Domain and you just don't like doing them, you're far more likely to get distracted.

Once you've automated, eliminated, or delegated everything from your Gravitational Domain, get Inertial Domain tasks off your plate.

Potential Energy Domain

Potential Energy describes tasks that you're good at and like doing, but they don't bring you the most joy. They have the potential to make you money but not as much as other tasks have. For example, for me, a Potential Energy task would be something like setting up ads. I enjoyed it, but it's no longer the best, most profitable use of my time.

The longer you keep Potential Domain tasks on your plate, the longer it will take for you to scale. While you can give tasks in the Potential Domain 90 percent, someone else can give them 100% and are at their happiest and most fulfilled and successful when they do those tasks. And it's that 10% that makes a substantial difference to your bottom line.

Fair warning: This is probably going to be the part of the energy domains that you have the most resistance to, because unlike the others, you don't hate doing these tasks. They're fine. And you'll have a harder time justifying giving up a task you like doing to someone who *loves* doing it. Your ego account will definitely take a hit when you see what the extra 10% looks like.

Ultimately, the team did the tasks just as well if not better than I did. It was a blow to realize the team didn't need me to do them, but I had to reframe it as a win: I had built a team that was so effective, it could run without me. That freed me up to do only a few tasks—my favorite ones—that nobody but me could do. That's also when Yves and I actually started being able to really enjoy our lives and prioritize the lifestyle we wanted.

Potential Domain tasks tend to be higher-dollar tasks. They are usually hard to automate; most of them require some sort of human intervention.

They're also the ones you can step back into. For example, if a team member was sick or on vacation and no one else was available, it was no problem for me to step in. It was a good money-making activity for that day.

That also means that these tasks should be the last ones you outsource. They're worth taking on when a temporary need arises. But when you do have to step back into them, you'll quickly realize that they've become Inertial tasks.

Kinetic Energy Domain

Kinetic energy is the energy of action and motion. This applies to the tasks that you're great at and that you absolutely love. When you're in your "Kinetic Domain," you don't feel like you're working. You might even feel guilty doing these tasks because they're such a joy.

For me, this includes things like content creation, marketing strategy, and overall business strategy. I could do these things all day long. They don't drain my energy; they create it.

These are also the highest-leverage business tasks. They probably don't require you to *do* a whole lot, but only to direct. Directors are essential to a film, even though you see only the actors on the screen; it's the directors' vision that brings things to life. This domain includes vision, the strategic direction, and partnerships—things that can only be done by you, and your team will follow your lead.

Over time, you might be able to delegate even some of these tasks to your team so that only the most essential things fall to you. *That's* freedom.

MASTER OF YOUR DOMAIN

Now, imagine if you were operating in your Kinetic Domain all day. You would never have to drag yourself to do something. You wouldn't have things put in front of you that don't activate you in an energizing way—all those sticky, pebbly areas from your other three domains that require things like coffee and motivation.

What if you could set up your operations in such a way that even your team members recognized when you weren't doing something in your Kinetic Domain and took it off your hands because the task was in *theirs*?

This is where the Energy Audit is key.

The 7-Figure Agent Starter Kit contains an Energy Audit template, as well as an instructional video so you understand how to use it. Use this audit to start taking things off your plate. Start with the things that you don't like and you're not good at. Eliminating those *alone* will actually give you back a lot of your energy.

Then take off the tasks that you don't like but are good at because, being good at them, you can likely train someone else to do them.

The things you're good at and that you like but don't excite you are usually higher level, more important functions, so you can save those for last. Those tasks will be the hardest for you to delegate and will be your hardest role to fill. The person to take those tasks will likely be a CEO or COO in your organization. Make no mistake—the biggest opportunity for business growth lies in your ability to free up energy in your day. Stop thinking in terms of time management; instead think in terms of energy management. It's easy to get into the practice of "do, do, do," hustle and grind—but you've got to be hyper-aware of what you're working on throughout the day and then checking in to see whether or not you're actually in your Kinetic Domain.

It might go against your principles to hire someone for tasks you feel you have the time and space to complete yourself. That's limited thinking, though. The truth is that most people who are true entrepreneurs and visionaries need as much free time as possible.

For instance, if I have two or three hours during which I'm able to just sit and think instead of being productive just so I can *feel* productive, I will come up with something that's either going to save or make my business money. Having unstructured time to think and create is incredibly important. There's a reason why your best ideas come to you while you're driving, in the shower, or falling asleep. It's because your brain is disconnected.

Perform a full Energy Audit, both professional and personal. The more efficient you are, the more you will get done and the more free time you will have. This goes not only for you, but for everyone on your team, as well. The idea is to make every aspect of your business and personal life free of wasted time and energy.

Write down everything you do in a day for a week. And I do mean *everything*—how many times you check your email, how many times you're interrupted by your phone—all of it. Honesty is key here. Once you've done this, parse each of these items into the four domains I've described above.

Then determine which of these things can be eliminated, automated, or outsourced. Anything leftover stays on your plate.

For example, delegate tasks that you love to do—whether that's sales or designing marketing collateral or answering customer-service emails—to other people who can do those tasks efficiently and at a high level. The ROI on that decision is always positive.

I learned long ago that there is zero point in holding on to certain tasks at the cost of efficiency or simply for the sake of holding on to them. Again, think bank account versus ego account! Holding on to them might feed your ego account, but it won't fill your bank account.

HOW MUCH YOU MAKE VERSUS HOW MUCH YOU KEEP

Elimination and automation must come before outsourcing.

There are a number of people who make a lot of money—but they don't actually keep very much of it.

Let's say you need a certain task off your plate and you decide you're going to pay someone $20 an hour to do it for twenty hours per week. But software or technology can do it for a monthly fee of $125.

If you make that one-time investment in automation instead of defaulting to weekly outsourcing, you maximize the time and efficiency of each person on your team. Those twenty hours are now freed up for that person to work on something that potentially generates more revenue for the business.

However, don't make the mistake of thinking that because you have a customer relationship management (CRM) system for your business, you've got automation. A CRM is the bare minimum —it's essentially just client management. True automation comes in the form of software like Zapier, which integrates your emails with your CRM and allows for the automation based on certain triggers.

Add to that SAAS companies like Airtable for team and transaction management, and ClickUp for project management, all with high levels of automation, and you'll have a streamlined business.

As just one example, in our 7-Figure Agent Collective mastermind, when a team lead wants to hire a new team member, we have an Airtable database template set up so that all the team lead has to do is customize a set of emails with call-booking links and update the status of applications. There is even a pre-created, modifiable form for candidates to fill out.

The system takes care of everything else—asking people to book appointments, distributing next steps to candidates moving forward, sending rejection emails, and more. The team lead spends time only on the important things that cannot be automated: interviewing, reviewing sample tasks, and sending a customized offer letter to the final candidate.

That's automation. If our members had to manually send out each email to each person, hiring would take twice as long and involve a lot more digging and repetition. If they outsourced those tasks to an agency, they'd be paying far more money than for the software and technology we use to get the tasks completed.

From contract to close, you should have a systematized process for everything that happens and in what order. There should be things that happen automatically through pieces of software and technology to maximize efficiency while keeping more of your hard-earned revenue in your pocket.

STANDARD OPERATING PROCEDURES

When the time comes for you to outsource, you must have standard operating procedures (SOP) for everything you want that person to do.

The purpose of an SOP is to provide detailed instructions about how to carry out a task so that any team member can do it correctly every time. It is critical to have every one of those tasks documented because once you document them, other people can follow them.

Once you have your SOPs clearly and concisely documented, it is so much easier to train new employees, and delegate or outsource tasks. If there's ever any question about how to do a particular job, team members or vendors can pull up the SOP document and video to understand what needs to be done. Having SOPs saves time and money, and creates better communication within your business.

There is a very simple template to creating an SOP. And yes, we have a template for you to use in the 7-Figure Agent Starter Kit (the free training course at the end of this book).

The SOP should have a title, a date of creation, the department name, and the owner of the document. If the SOP is about commissions or finances, someone who deals with those areas of the business should own the document. Also include when the document was last updated, so that you always know if it's out of date.

Include clear action steps that are accurate or that apply to 95 percent of cases. I can't emphasize enough how important clarity is. It is incredibly inefficient for team members to come to you every single time they have a question about something they don't understand. When they come to you for everything, you just become an assistant to the rest of your team. Clear, actionable SOPs take that off your plate.

Include in your SOP how to know when a task is completed. Also, link any documents, media, or references associated with that task, including email templates and passwords.

Once you've created the SOP document, place it in an accessible location, and make sure your entire team knows where to find it. We have our SOPs in our project management software. You can also place it in a Google Drive accessible to the whole team.

Create a tracker (or playbook), which is essentially a table of contents of all of the SOPs you create. This allows people to search by department or SOP title to find what they need quickly. The idea is to make these answers as accessible as possible to, again, remove responding to procedural questions from your daily leadership responsibilities.

Having SOPs not only makes operations more efficient, but it also means that your training of new employees is more consistently excellent. If you experience churn on your team, you don't have to keep personally training them. That's especially true if you've created a video overview of all tasks and procedures, along with a written document that lists the people who are involved in each task.

To make the videos, use a screen recording software (I recommend Loom) so that when you're creating a new SOP, you can go through the task on the computer and record what you're doing so a trainee can easily follow along. This covers people who are visual learners or who need to review instructions a few times.

Yes, your SOPs will take time to set up, but once you've done them, you'll be amazed at the amount of time you get back in your day to commit yourself to the tasks your business needs you—and only you—to do.

A FUNDAMENTAL CHANGE

When I realized the importance of operations and made the necessary changes, I was brought back to why I got into the business in the first place.

I finally had the ability to generate unlimited income. There was no ceiling because I had all of the systems dialed in, including unlimited scalability from a marketing standpoint.

I could breathe. That breathing room allowed me to have more impact and help more people with a consistent level of excellent service instead of giving them less than the best of me. I had freedom. I started traveling more and spending a lot more time with my family. I was able to take more time off because I was comfortable with my team running things.

Speaking of teams...we're finally at the promised land!

Chapter Seven

PILLAR SIX:
TEAM HIRING AND LEADERSHIP

I built the wrong team before I built the right team.

One day, I looked around and realized that I was essentially the assistant to everyone on my team. I was serving them, and not in the way my team talks about servant leadership today. I was doing all the things no one else wanted to do—the work from *their* Gravitational Domains—and cleaning up all of their messes. If a team member told me they didn't have time to complete a task, I did it. I was still operating with the mentality that this was my business, and no one would care for it the way I would.

Looking back, my first mistake was that I hired when I was desperate. I waited until it hurt—until I was essentially at a breaking point. Then I would hire in haste—the opposite of the best advice, which is to hire slow and fire fast.

I was gullible. When people told me they had skill sets, I didn't do the background work to ensure they actually had them. I was so desperate that I just took people at their word that they could do the job. As you can guess, that wasn't the case.

Because I was always waiting until the last minute to grow, I wound up with people who weren't in value-alignment with me. We call this "culture fit." They didn't share my values in terms of how to speak with clients, how much to push them, and what our actual processes were.

I found myself with someone on my team with whom I became extremely close, but who was incredibly pushy with clients and terribly disorganized—not to mention the fact that her schedule didn't work with what I was trying to do, and she eventually seemed to care less and less about the quality of her work.

Seems obvious that you should fire someone who is doing a poor job, is not meeting their key performance indicators (KPIs), and is a poor fit with the company's values, right? Of course, that isn't what I did.

I was afraid to let her go because by now I knew for sure that I couldn't do everything on my own. I thought that if I had at least *some* help I could make the rest work. All that did was put me in the middle of a big mess.

I was so afraid, in fact, that I kept this assistant on for a *year*.

If poor hiring that you won't correct is not your situation, congratulations. But I'm willing to bet you know at least one agent with an admin you absolutely hate dealing with. That's because *so* many agents hire out of desperation. They wait until they are in so much pain that they end up with the wrong people—either the wrong people on the team or in the wrong roles.

You should not hire the first person you find until that person proves to be the best option compared with the candidates you find next. Even then, if you're not convinced, start the process again. Don't settle.

We also tend to hire people we like. When you hire people you like, you find yourself with a team of people who are essentially just like you, which is *not* what you want. When you're building a team, you want people who fill in the gaps you leave. As an example, often agents are either good with clients or with the backend of the business dealings. If you're one or the other, you need the opposite.

Everyone can find amazing, high-quality team members. You just have to know how.

GET HONEST

Make an honest assessment about where you're strong and where you aren't, much like the Energy Audit exercise in the previous chapter. Doing so will give you a much clearer perspective on your actual needs and the skill sets you're looking for.

Make sure you're using the right tools. For hiring at The Listings Lab, we—and our clients—use a full personality and striving instincts assessment. We recommend the Kolbe-A assessment, which tells how someone is going to act when they're free to be themselves; and the Love Languages test, which shows how people like to receive praise, feedback, and affirmation.

At the end of the day, building the right team is about hiring the right people (before you get desperate) and putting them in the right roles: Make sure that they have the ability, the capacity, and the desire to sit in the seat you're offering them within your business.

You Might Not Be a Leader

Frequently in real estate, the people who end up as team leaders do not have leadership backgrounds. If that's you, and you're not a good leader, you'll need to develop leadership skills or you will lose good people. Great team members want to feel like they're part of a team. They want to feel supported as well as to provide support. They want to know what they're working towards and feel connected to that goal.

One of the biggest ways poor leadership shows up is by outsourcing the task of leadership. Again, if that describes your behavior, you might try to justify it by assuming, if you haven't done it before or well, that it's in your Gravitational Domain. But for you and your team to thrive, leadership absolutely needs to be in your Kinetic Domain.

Great team members want to feel like they're part of a team. They want to feel supported as well as to provide support. They want to know what they're working towards and feel connected to that goal. That's the result of great leadership, and it's a skill you need to cultivate if you haven't already done so.

You cannot outsource your leadership. You can have team members manage the day-to-day of the team. But the big decisions and the hard conversations? Those need to come from you. Someone needs to be steering the ship, and that someone has to be you. You can find a lot of value from authors like Brené Brown and Simon Sinek if this is a skill you want to refine.

Hire A-Players

To use a baseball analogy, push for talent outside of your league because A-players understand the role, want the role, and have the capacity to do the role better than other people. These players might be more expensive, but they always provide the biggest return on your investment. (What's more, A-players often introduce you to other A-players, which helps you to create a world-class team.)

A-players care deeply about your business and your mission. They motivate and uplift other people on your team, which also helps with the culture. Because you're not hiring someone straight out of college who has to look to you for everything, your A-players are actually going to push you out of your comfort zone to be your best. From the moment they join, A-players are all in. Unlike people looking for a side hustle while they build their own thing, they're fully committed to you and your business.

My COO, Ashley, whom I affectionately call the other half of my life, is the epitome of an A-player. Outside of being one of the most organized people I've ever met and having a phenomenal memory (she's like a personal Google for the company), she treats my business like it's her own—not from a place of ego but from a place of care.

As our primary project manager and the person whose job it is to spot inefficiencies and redundancies in our business and correct them, she holds our team to a high standard, and she expects excellence from everyone. But she's also the first person to give praise and recognition for a job well done. She sets the expectation for the team of what it means to work for us, and she makes sure that not only do we complete the projects we set, she usually sneaks in a few extra ones in every quarter. My job as a CEO is a thousand times easier because I have her in my corner.

You want people who treat your business that way, from your eventual right-hand down to your runner who delivers paperwork and does pickups. When you have A-players on your team, your primary job is to make sure their lives run as smoothly as possible, not to introduce an agent who makes them less efficient and changes their experience of working for and with you.

Another reason not to wait to hire until you're desperate is that the top-level people you need are not always easy to find, so you need to give yourself time. If instead you rush and don't hire an A-player, you plunge the lives of the A-players on your team into chaos.

FIVE HIRING STAGES

There are five stages to hiring A-players: preparation, recruitment, interview, trial period, and hiring and onboarding.

Preparation

Most people in real estate are flying by the seat of their pants when it comes to hiring. They know they need an assistant, but they have no idea what they're specifically looking for. They only know they need help.

The biggest thing that keeps new hires from performing well is not having a clear role with clear expectations. That happens because the hiring agent did not prepare for recruitment. You need to have an ironclad Roles and Responsibilities document that helps you identify the kind of help you need and that will allow you to clearly communicate your expectations to candidates throughout the hiring process.

You need an actual hiring process with a timeline. An example is a test (more on that in the next section) or a screening call for a hiring interview.

Also, when I said not to rush into hiring, that means at *least* two weeks to find a viable candidate. For more complicated jobs, you might need longer. You want a fairly large sample of candidates to be able to have the cream rise to the top in an obvious way.

Once you've got the Roles and Responsibilities done with a time-line in place, you have to create an application. Don't just ask candidates to send a resume. Create an actual application that candidates must fill out because you want someone who has taken the time to understand the role and fill out the application, not someone who's carpet bombing their CV all over the place.

At The Listings Lab, one of our most effective ways to screen is to ask applicants to follow these instructions:

1. Fill out the application thoroughly, and

2. Shoot a 2-minute video telling us why you would be an asset to our team, upload it to YouTube as an unlisted video, and email the link to our hiring manager.

Right away, this weeds out 50 percent of applicants who don't submit a video or who do it incorrectly because if people can't read simple instructions, they don't belong on the team. You need people who, at the very least, can follow instructions to the letter.

At a bare minimum, give an application, test, then interview.

Recruitment

Start recruitment with people who are familiar with your market and what you do. Your number-one source is always referrals. Ask your network, team members, employees, and clients, "Who is the best person you know at 'X' role?" You can also go to your current audience via social media, email, newsletters, and the like. Your third option is online job boards.

Send that pool of people your application and a test that you've designed to weed people out. Look for things like attention to detail, level of care, mistakes, level of desire, skills, culture fit, and the ability to problem-solve. Depending on the role, this process should trim the list down to three to five people.

Interview

Everyone's interview questions are likely to be a bit different, but your list should always include these three:

"Why is this the job for you?"

"What are your goals?"

"Why did you leave your last job?"

You also want to use those questions and others to look into whether the candidate

- truly understands the position. Are they on the same page about what the role actually is? If they can describe the role back to you in a way that closely mirrors what you would say, then they get it. But if the clarity isn't there, you *can't* move on to the next step. Address that right away.

- actually wants the role. Are they hungry and motivated? Sometimes, people will temporarily sit in a role they don't want, and it's a house of cards. They'll either leave soon after they're hired, or they'll be frustrated in their role and you won't get the best out of them. You want someone who gets up every morning wanting to do their job. You can't pay or motivate someone to want it. The desire for the role already has to be there. If you bump someone's pay, the increase might motivate them briefly, but it's not a long-term solution.

▸ has the necessary skill set to understand the role and what's necessary to succeed in it.

▸ is open-minded, coachable, and excited to learn from you.

▸ is honest and direct with their responses, particularly about why they left (or were fired from) their last job.

▸ is clear about the direction they want to go and why they feel this is the right time for this position.

▸ has income goals that are in line with what the position will provide.

Also look at capacity. Does the person have the time, the expertise, and the mental, physical, and emotional capacity to do the job? And do they have the time? Or will their life commitments consistently keep them from the weekly hours you need from them?

Skills and expertise, however, aren't necessarily a deal killer. Skills can be trained—as long as you or someone on your staff has the time or patience to bring them to the level you require. If you don't, recognize that, and don't settle for anyone who does not have full capacity from the get-go.

Throughout the interview, watch out for red flags, including speaking poorly of past bosses, being focused only on the money, or having no idea about your market. Also steer clear if they don't mention any past failures or areas where they can improve, or if they generally have a bad attitude or are overly confident.

Trial Period

Far too many people hire without a paid trial period.

If you're hiring for a full-time role, the non-negotiable trial period should be thirty to sixty days. If you skip or shorten it, you will suffer the consequences. The trial period needs to be long enough to ensure that you're not seeing a new hire on only their best behavior, which would be hard to sustain. Sooner or later they're bound to slip out of their best behavior. Pay attention to that, and see it as the red flag it is.

If after their trial period, someone meets their KPIs and proves to be a good culture fit, onboard them. If not, go back to stage one.

Onboarding

During onboarding, set clear expectations about both the company's communication rhythm and the position. Give your new hires honest feedback about what they've done well in their first month or two with the company, as well as where they still have strides to make. You can't expect someone to improve if you don't clearly tell them that they aren't meeting a specific expectation.

Are there weekly reports and check-ins? Is there a quarterly review? What are their performance goals? Talk about salary, performance, and role reviews at the six-month mark.

If someone is going to stay with you, invest in their performance with outside courses and consultants. And check in with your team members personally. If their excitement fades over time or they outgrow the position they were hired for, it's time to move them to another role that does get them excited about their job.

SCORECARDS

Empower your team. There is a big difference between delegating tasks and delegating outcomes. For example, you can make someone responsible for the outcome of doubling the number of referrals to your company in that fiscal year. It's then up to them to figure out just how to do that.

The role scorecard should clearly lay out the following:

- the person's position

- who they report to

- the required skills, knowledge, and traits to be successful in the position

- the KPIs they are responsible for in the business

- the duties of the role and how frequently they are to be performed

Essentially, everyone needs to know what key outcomes they have to produce. All too often, people run down their checklists each day without owning any outcomes.

Over time, you can change the KPIs for any role. In a quarterly check-in with your team, evaluate the performance of team members, make sure they are ROI-positive, and deliver both positive and constructive feedback to your team about how they can improve and be better accountable to their KPIs.

The quarterly check-in is also when you set the success metrics for that quarter. If , say, referrals were successfully doubled, do you want to maintain that or shoot for an even bigger goal?

Every team member should know what their responsibilities are, what their KPIs are, and what success metrics they are expected to be meeting. Essentially, everyone needs to know what key outcomes they have to produce. All too often, people run down their checklists each day without owning any outcomes.

The scorecard ensures these expectations are communicated in writing and delivered to team members. When they are onboarded, it should be one of the first things they see.

MISTAKES TO AVOID

Some of these common mistakes might seem self-explanatory, but they're worth reviewing.

Hiring is one of the easiest and best ways to scale your business. But don't hire until you've worn all the hats and are familiar with every single aspect of your business. Hiring too soon will eat up your cash reserves because you don't actually understand every part of your business well enough to bring in someone else to handle parts of it. That means you won't know how to direct them in the right way.

For instance, you need to understand marketing before you can outsource it. If you don't you'll end up with people who perform poorly, and you won't be clear on what to do about it.

When you find that you're stuck in a hamster wheel and relatively maxed out, it's time to do an Energy Audit—looking at your daily tasks to determine what roles to hire for first. Again, only hire when you've identified the things you want and need off your plate.

You won't have to worry about your expenses growing before your revenue does if you don't hire too quickly and if you delegate appropriately. Every person you bring onto your team should have an ROI, and they should know and understand what their expected ROI over time is. Even an assistant will add a certain amount of money to your bottom line if they're freeing you up for income-generating activities. The rule of thumb is that if you pay an assistant $40,000 per year, they should be adding a minimum of $60,000 per year to the bottom line.

ORDER OF HIRING

It will become clear whom you need and when. When you do a full Energy Audit, you'll start seeing things that are outside your Kinetic Domain taking up time and energy. That's when you know it's time to look for either a software or a person who can take these tasks off your plate and start owning those outcomes.

I recommend that your first hire be a part-time virtual assistant (VA) or a contractor who does small, routine admin tasks. Delegating these tasks can free up anywhere from ten to thirty hours of your time per week. There are a lot of VA sourcing companies you can enlist for help; get a referral for a high-quality option.

From there, you can progress to taking on full-time virtual contractors. They're typically young people or hustling work-from-home moms who will do whatever's necessary to get the job done and move the needle forward. You might not have these roles really well defined until you see what you need done.

But don't mistake a virtual jack-of-all-trades who is in a more entry-level position for someone who's not an A-player. Their level also doesn't mean your expectations should be less. If you've gone through the five stages of hiring properly, you'll always find someone who is clearly the best fit. Sometimes you'll even end up with two. That's where things like skills assessments, references, and accuracy and speed of trial tasks can play a deciding role.

Some of these contractors are likely to get a look at your systems and help you revamp some things along the way. In that case, you might bump them from being a part-time VA to your full-time administrator. Your admin probably doesn't need to be local. If you really need a local person, ask yourself if there are really two jobs being crammed into one person's workload.

Your third hire should be a full-time person who has specialized knowledge you need. These roles include buyer's agents, operations managers, listing specialists, and others. It's smart to make sure they have numbers they need to hit. They need to know that they're accountable to the KPIs you set for them.

These are people who will bring in more money and not cost you any, with the exception of an operations manager. (But even they will free up a lot of your time for those high-value tasks). You'll want to find these people via referrals or social media.

CULTURE: CORE VALUES AND CAPES

Hire—and fire—according to the core values and purpose of the business.

Core values are your company's timeless guiding principles. Choose three to seven values and use them to hire, fire, review, reward, and recognize people on your team. They are the foundation to a thriving team culture. The specific methodologies for creating a set of core values go beyond the scope of this book, but, as an example, let's look at my business's core values. They are represented by the acronym CAPES because all of our team members are superheroes.

C is for **Clear and Compassionate Communication.** Nothing is left unsaid. We communicate when something is needed or wrong. This removes drama and resentment while creating transparency. We list behaviors that support this value, as well as behaviors that are the antithesis of each of those behaviors.

A is for **Always Celebrating.** We celebrate personal and business wins because it creates a culture of positivity and fun. We take our work seriously—but not necessarily ourselves. If someone has amazing things happening in their personal or professional life and they're not sharing it, they're "win hoarding." That goes against our culture.

P is for **Personal Responsibility.** This value is all about ownership and removing victimhood. There is no blaming. If we drop the ball, we take ownership. If we make a mistake, we come up with solutions. If we're stressed and need help, it's our responsibility to raise our hand and ask for help.

E is for **Evolutionary Growth.** Having a growth mindset at all times benefits us all because it pushes our boundaries as human beings. Instead of taking feedback personally, we use it to inquire about how we can grow and improve. Then both the business and the team grow.

S is for **Servant Leadership.** This value is not about martyrdom. We operate from a win-win mindset. We don't support ideas that are not in the greatest interest of everyone involved. No secret personal agendas are allowed. We serve our clients, community, team—everyone—from a place of abundance, not scarcity. Every decision has to be a win for us *and* them.

Having these well-established core values allows us to fall back on them when someone behaves in a manner that violates those values. If they're unable to get back in alignment with the values, it's clear that they're not a culture fit, and it may be time for them to move on. If someone is consistently violating one or more core values, they get a warning. After that, it's a terminable offense.

That said, if the issue is that the right person is in the wrong seat, we look for another role for them within the company. Make no mistake, the right person for the culture is critical to the success of the team.

If you're going to hold your team to core values you've created, you have to commit to them. You can't ask people to be clear communicators and then walk around the office being passive-aggressive or snapping at people all day.

Discuss your core values weekly, quarterly, and at every review. Whenever you give someone feedback, ground it in the core values.

As important as the core values are to the success of your business, so too are the mission and vision of your company. In fact, an aligned mission, vision, and core values are the perfect trifecta of a successful culture.

Chapter Eight

PILLAR SEVEN: VISIONING

Though many of us got into real estate for unlimited income potential, flexibility of schedule, and the chance to make an impact in people's lives, the truth is that many of us lose sight of those goals. If you've lost sight of them, it's okay. You're going to uncover how to get back on track.

You should know you've lost sight of them when all you care about is the next deal. That mentality can become ingrained. Sure, there's a little bit of business planning here and there, but one day, maybe decades into your career, you wake up and ask yourself:

What happened? How did I get here? How did my priorities and my life plan become so unbalanced?

When you first got started in real estate, you probably loved that rush of a closed deal. Who wouldn't? It's fun. But eventually, you have to realize that you can't build a life on the highs and lows of the deal chase.

Your business was created to serve your life, not the other way around. If you live to serve your business, you're going to be enslaved to it because you're operating without intentionality. You haven't done any visioning work, and so you have no idea where you're going. You're running your business day to day, quarter by quarter.

When I speak with agents, I'll ask them in November about their plans for the coming year. Almost every time, they tell me that they haven't done their goal setting for next year. They are invariably the ones whose businesses are running their lives and not the other way around. They're stuck.

While entrepreneurs are visionaries, *visioning* is the number-one thing that many business owners overlook. It's often because they constantly and consistently live in a scarcity mindset grounded in a world with a short attention span. The real estate industry as a whole is relatively unpredictable. We're at the mercy of market changes, seasons, interest rates, and government decisions. As a result, most agents run their business by simply putting one foot in front of the other.

But your vision is also the number-one thing that can move the needle forward in your business. When you have a solid, compelling vision, not only does it help you attract A-players for your team, but it also helps you dominate your marketplace.

Successful agents, team leaders, and organizations not only have a compelling vision, but they effectively communicate it to both their teams and their market. This means they're able to attract, inspire, and motivate their team. But what does visioning actually mean?

CORE COMPONENTS

Visioning is made up of six components: core values, core purpose, ten-year target, three-year picture, one-year plan, and quarterly rocks (concrete, attainable goals). There are step-by-step processes for nailing down each one.

Core Values

As you learned in the previous chapter, core values are the foundation to building a thriving culture within your organization. By telling people in your company what you stand for as a business, they can base their decisions on those values. And that means you don't need to be available to answer every single little question. Core values also determine practices for hiring and firing, reviews, rewards, and recognition.

Core Purpose

Once you've got your core values dialed in, your core purpose comes next.

Do not feel pressure to nail your core purpose down right away. It's normal if it takes you some time to figure it out. Your core purpose is why you do what you do and why it matters.

For example, as I mentioned, I felt so alone as I tried to get my real estate business off the ground. It wasn't until I started building my own tribe, when I found people that cared about me and cared about my success, that I was able to truly see what was possible. It was then that I realized that connecting with others was the core purpose of my business. And when I transitioned into The Listings Lab, the core became helping agents to build relationships at scale.

You have to have a central idea about why you do what you do. Then, to bring people into your world, you have to tell a story around that idea. This is your brand story, the origin story of who you are, where you came from, and why you're here today doing what you do. It should help people to understand your core purpose.

Your brand story should also increase the amount your audience both likes and trusts you. A lot of agents only care about seeming credible and professional with their brand. Of course, those qualities are important, but the vital piece most agents get very wrong—if not completely ignore—is likeability.

When your clients see you as an authority, that means they trust you to provide a service—but they don't want to buy those services from a robot. They want to buy them from a person. Whether or not those clients like you as a person plays a huge part in whether or not they choose you as their agent—and keep choosing you, as well as telling their friends to choose you.

But you can't communicate your likeability as a bulleted list of benefits. Let's face it—any time we see someone list a bunch of great adjectives about themselves, the less likely we are to like that person. So, the best and only way to communicate your true likeability?

That's right—your brand story.

Ten-Year Target

The ten-year target is actually very simple—where do you want your organization to be a decade from now?

A universally common thread among successful people is that they have a habit of setting and achieving goals. If you're not clear about where your ship is going, how do you expect to steer toward what you want?

The ten-year target is your North Star. It's your "big, hairy, audacious goal," as Jim Collins put it in his book *Built to Last*. To create that target, meet with your core team to discuss where you want to take the business. First, ask them where they believe the organization could be in ten years—it should be something crazy. The whole idea here is to inspire the hell out of everyone on your team to hit that goal. The goal shouldn't just be revenue-based. Maybe some aspect of social change could come as a result of the revenue earned.

Whatever the goal, it should be something that gets everyone motivated and inspired. It should make everyone believe they have a purpose—and that they know where everyone is going.

Three-Year Picture

Now get a bit more granular with what you and the team expect the company to look like and to have achieved in three years. This is designed for everyone on your team and in your orbit to see what you're saying so they can figure out whether they want to be a part of that vision.

The three-year picture is a terrific recruiting tool. It helps you ask: "Do you want to be a part of an organization that looks like this in three years?" If a candidate's answer is no, you know immediately that they won't be a good fit.

Why three years? There is little value in detailed strategic planning more than three years out. Yes, you still do the ten-year target because you want to know where the ship is heading. But a vivid three-year picture will let your organization attract top-quality team members and drive what all agents want, which is market domination. When your three-year picture is clear, it improves your one-year planning process because you can more easily determine what you have to do over the next twelve months to stay on track for the three-year picture.

The first step in developing this picture is to spend at least an hour with your core team to determine what the annual revenue will be in three years (keeping in mind what you already determined it would be for the ten-year target). The answers will fall in a range, but you need to settle on one number. Note: If you're a solo agent, it's also fine to create this picture by yourself.

Next, agree on the profit number. This is a similar discussion, but it should go much quicker. For instance, if you expect to do $5 million in revenue in three years, how much of that do you expect to be profit?

Then determine specific measurables unique to your team. Number of clients, number of units, and price points are all examples.

Different markets will have different numbers and different categories of importance.

Next, everyone on the core team should create their "painting." Ask them to write down bullet points to describe what the organization will look like three years from now. They should consider the number and quality of people on the team, added resources, office size, systems and technology leads, and client mix. Once everyone has painted this picture individually, bring them all together to choose ten to twenty bullet points that make up your three-year picture.

Finally, crystallize the picture, so that everyone has absolute clarity on it.

Also, ask the team to regularly engage in this exercise. It's going to sound a little touchy-feely, but it works by pulling everyone towards the goal. Have them close their eyes and visualize that three-year picture. Ask them to feel what it would be like to have that picture come to fruition.

One-Year Plan

The one-year plan brings the long-range vision down to earth and makes it real. It makes your three-year and ten-year goals possible. And it's simple to establish.

The best way to do this is with a two-hour team meeting. I know all of this seems to require a lot of meetings, but they're worth it because they remove the possibility of people not being on the same page. Hold the one-year plan meeting at the end of the current year you're in, even if you're planning in the middle of the year, so everyone's on the same schedule.

In this meeting, determine your revenue picture by asking your team to estimate the annual revenue one year from that day. Once again, the answers will range, but pick a number. Then, as before, agree on the profit number. Both answers should fall in line with your three-year picture. You'll also determine the specific measurables, keeping them aligned with your long-term picture and target.

Set up three to seven priorities or goals to hit your longer-term goals. If you make everything important, then nothing is important, so don't create too many priorities. Those priorities should be what *has* to be completed this year for you to be on track for your three-year picture.

As with any other goals, these must be SMART: specific, measurable, attainable, realistic, and timed. "More sales" is not a specific goal. $100 million in sales is, so is hiring a virtual assistant by the end of Q3. Setting unrealistic goals is the biggest trap people fall into in these exercises. When they miss them, it throws them off track for their long-term goals.

By the way, if you're a solo agent, you can perform these exercises. Find an accountability partner if necessary and go through all of these with them.

Quarterly Rocks

Next, set rocks—ninety-day priorities and goals to keep you on track for your one-year plan.

The rock metaphor comes from author Gino Wickman, and it's one of my favorites. The idea is you start with an empty jar. Throughout the quarter, the jar gets filled with your day-to-day activities, represented by sand, water, and mud. However, if you don't put in your priorities—the rocks—*first*, they won't fit in the jar and they won't get done.

At the start of every quarter, put in three to five rocks for your best chance of hitting those goals, which feed into your one-year plan, and so on. Establishing these priorities lets you maintain focus even when other situations can—and do—arise. You can still have new ideas and try new things, but get those three to five things done first, and everything else after that is gravy.

Again, assemble your core team for a one- to two-hour meeting that starts with a brain dump about everything you want to close out in the next ninety days. The list can be anywhere from ten to twenty items. Then make a decision on each one—do you kill it, keep it, or combine it as a quarterly rock.

Narrow it down to no fewer than three rocks and no more than five. Then set the dates when the rocks are due.

Make the quarterly rock objectives super clear, and like other goals, SMART. A good example of a quarterly rock is hiring a new buyer's agent. A bad example is starting work on the referral process.

Each of the rocks has to be owned by one person on the team. That doesn't mean they have to complete the goal alone, but they are in charge of making sure that the result happens. At the end of the quarter, if a rock didn't get completed, you need to know whom to hold accountable.

Create a sheet for use in your weekly meetings to reconnect to your rocks and determine whether you're on track. We use Airtable to list all of our rocks, their owners, their due dates, and their status. We use ClickUp to manage the individual projects that ensure that rock is completed. During every meeting, address the rocks and your progress towards them.

GIVE YOURSELF SPACE

Visioning allows you to create the life and business you actually want. Some people think that, to figure out all of these components, they need to take a massive break from their business. The truth is you don't need to disappear on a weeks-long retreat—but you do need a small amount of distance to be effective in determining your vision.

This is because a vision is something that comes not only from your head, but also your heart. If you don't give yourself a little bit of distance from your business, you might not see clearly where it is you want to be. Sometimes, we try to vision from a place of burnout, and that's never going to give us a clear picture.

I can't emphasize enough how important clarity is to your vision.

Vision drives your goals.

Goals drive your planning.

Planning drives your resources.

Resources drive your execution.

Execution drives your results.

Your results will become more natural when they come from a place of vision. So often we build for the sake of building. When you do this, you'll end up resentful of your business or fall off track, and you won't even care because your vision wasn't created from a real place.

So, give yourself that space to work out your vision. The more detailed you can be, the better results you'll achieve.

Personal Vision

We detailed how to create a vision for your business—but what about for yourself?

Just as in business, start looking ten years out—and you really want to stretch yourself. This should be an uncomfortable exercise. You should say to yourself, "I would need to become a completely different person to get there."

Basic categories to consider when it comes to your personal vision include finances, family, faith, business, fitness, and team. No matter how you organize these categories, you want to create a vision that inspires you. Some people organize their vision in bullet points; others write it down in a stream of consciousness.

Once you have it clear in your mind what this vision looks and feels like, work backwards. Establish your ten-year vision. Then create a realistic but high-aiming three-year picture, which won't be as grand, but you can still accomplish a lot in that time.

Just as with your business, you'll then create a personal one-year plan. Where do you want to be on this date one year from now? The one-year plan should go toward helping you hit your three-year and ten-year targets.

When you're setting those targets, you need to be your own reality check. Without a doubt, this is the hardest part of this process. You have to be really honest about which of your habits are not serving you.

Are you watching three hours of television per day? Are you eating like crap? Are you spending money on things you don't need or that don't give you a return on investment? Does your three-year picture align with what you're doing today?

If you're not being painfully honest with yourself, there's no point in any of this; in a year, you'll be exactly where you are now, and if you're reading this book, I'm pretty sure that's not what you want. The only person you'll hurt by being dishonest is you. Getting real with yourself is the best thing you can do from a self-care perspective. When you've taken that hard internal look, then ask yourself: Who do I need to be to reach those goals and make my vision real?

Write down your new standard. Who are you going to be? What do you need to do? What are the new routines you need to adopt and the open loops you need to close? What are the hard conversations you're not having? Conversely, you also need to identify the things you wouldn't change because you probably don't have to change *everything* about yourself.

You also want to identify what your business goals mean for you personally. Then come up with five to seven projects that will help your business serve your personal life. When I did this, I hired a few additional people for my team so that I had more free time.

Then break these down into your personal rocks. What three to five projects are you going to work on for the next ninety days? Write down each task that will help you reach those goals.

Finally, which should come first, the personal or the professional vision? Personally, I prefer creating the personal vision first because it's too easy to get caught up in the excitement of numbers and revenue. I feel it's important to get grounded and clear on what you want your personal life to look and feel like—to decide what's truly important to you *outside* of your business so you can be happy in both your personal and professional life.

NOT THE SAME TWENTY-FOUR HOURS

You might be wondering why Visioning wasn't the first chapter.

When I outlined this book, it never occurred to me to put visioning first. I made this the final chapter because it's so important that I wanted it to be the final concept I left you with. I want you to truly understand that you are the captain of your ship instead of the victim of circumstances—pandemics, market swings, and so on.

But visioning is about radical personal responsibility. It's no one else on this planet's job to create the life that you want other than yourself.

You'll see memes that say things like, "Remember: Beyoncé also only has twenty-four hours in her day." Yes, but Beyoncé also has someone who does her hair, cooks her meals, and drives her around. Her twenty-four hours are nothing like yours. But if you want your twenty-four hours to look like hers, you can take steps to get there. I'm not saying you're going to be Beyoncé, but you *can* have a sustainable seven-figure business and a lot more free time.

People say to me all the time that they don't know how I get so much done. Well, I don't cook. I don't clean. I don't do laundry. I don't grocery-shop. My free time is spent as free time. I'm efficient because my time is sacred, and that was part of my vision. I wanted my twenty-four hours to be like no one else's.

When I started visioning as a solo agent, I saw immediate progress quarter by quarter. My rocks helped me sleep at night because I was no longer guessing, making things up, and flying by the seat of my pants. I knew that, to get me where I wanted to go, things needed to get done every quarter. Don't underestimate how freeing it is to take the guesswork out of everything.

With a few hours of planning, I stopped spitting spaghetti into napkins.

And that's priceless.

CONCLUSION

Pillars in Place

I've told you about how the system I've developed worked for me, but I also want to tell you about just one of the many real estate agents who has put these pillars in place to great success. For the sake of anonymity, we'll call this agent Justin.

Justin came to our program earning somewhere in the low six figures, but not seeing a lot of that money. He was stuck in the grind-and-hustle mode. The glorification of that mentality didn't speak to him, and he wanted to make sustainable changes to his business and personal life.

First, Justin worked on his *marketing,* and immediately began to see business growth through organic social media and paid traffic that increased his visibility. He was able to get in front of more and more people, using the psychology of "from stranger to client" and the notions of "know, like, and trust." So not only did Justin have a full pipeline, but he was building relationships at scale. He broke the real estate agent mold of one-to-one communication and converted to one-to-many. Every piece of content he created went to multiple people, creating several scalable "conversations."

But from a *mindset* standpoint, Justin was struggling. He was living in scarcity, both literally and figuratively. Even though his business was earning six figures, he had very little money in the bank. The program was a last stop for him. If it didn't work, his business was done. That fact was putting immense stress on his family life and friendships.

We wanted to remove that fear that things were going to stop working and have him step into a place where he believed that he was doing everything correctly and working toward reaching his goals. He had to believe things were going to go his way. His motivation could not be fear based.

Creating a *Signature System* was huge for Justin and his business. Having a named and branded system helped him advertise himself, but it also helped people look at him as an authority, someone who truly knew what he was doing. It said to potential clients that Justin had a proven system and methodology and that he specialized in helping them.

Then, when he started adding a team, his Signature System ensured that the level of service and execution was standardized, which made everything more scalable. People weren't saying, "Hey, I need Justin" because, in essence, they *were* getting Justin since he set the standard for how business was done throughout the team.

Sales conversations weren't so much a struggle for Justin as they were for his team. They had gotten so accustomed to scripts that their conversations with clients lacked any kind of personal touch and did not lead to relationships. A powerful business relationship is also a personal relationship. Selling and buying a home is an emotional decision, and you can't tap into those emotions if you're only developing a business relationship. Justin and his team learned how to create value in their conversations while also making their clients feel seen and understood.

Justin's *operations* were initially very disorganized on the back end. Even though he had someone in the business helping with the organizational side of things, the documents lived all over the place. He had just implemented a new CRM. He also had information in Google Drive. The team had a hard time tracking the conversations they were having.

Justin learned to simplify things and created an SOP for every situation. This returned a huge amount of time to his day because no longer was every single thing being threaded through him. His team had a lot more autonomy to work and build without running to him every time they had an issue.

Businesses have entrepreneurs, managers, and technicians. Just like the E-Myth[4] says, a lot of people in real estate are more technicians than entrepreneurs. But when you're first building a team, you have to sit in all three seats, which most people can't do well. When it came to *team hiring and leadership*, Justin was very entrepreneurial, but he'd been an agent for so long that he was used to micromanaging. He had been micromanaged and didn't really know any other way to lead.

Good leadership is being able to empower someone on your team to grow, learn, and expand. When they can do that, your business will grow as well. For Justin to accomplish this growth, some people had to be let go—but he also had existing people move into new roles because they demonstrated that they had a natural skill set that they didn't know about when they were first hired. Putting the right people in the right seats gave Justin the extra bandwidth to work *on* the business instead of *in* it.

Justin struggled with *visioning* because he was coming from a place of burnout and scarcity. Once he was able to shed that mindset, he reconnected with his love for not only the business, but also building the business. That allowed him to get clarity about where he really wanted to be—what his perfect day looked like in ten years, what he wanted his family life to look like, and what he wanted his business to look like.

---

[4] https://www.amazon.com/Myth-Most-Businesses-Dont-About/dp/0887303625

After eight months of implementing the pillars, Justin was well on his way to his first seven-figure year. He was so successful that he was able to look at operating in a second niche because he had so thoroughly dominated the market in his first one.

Justin went from losing himself in his business to turning both his life and company around.

And now it's your turn.

FOCUS BREEDS EXCELLENCE

The next step for you? Implement!

Start with an audit using each of the pillars in this book and decide which one you're going to focus on. Focus breeds excellence. If you try to implement all the pillars at once, you won't be successful. Tackle them one at a time by auditing your business and figuring out where you need to start.

Where is the most opportunity? Where are you going to find the quickest wins?

Then systematically move yourself through each of these pillars.

You don't have to do it alone. As a reader of this book, I invite you to The Listings Lab's Facebook group: The Listings Lab Method for Real Estate Agents. There you'll find free trainings to get you started on your path to seven figures. I hope to see you in there soon!

And don't forget to grab your 7-Figure Agent Starter Kit. (thelist ingslab.com/7fa). It's filled with worksheets, trainings, and guides to help you successfully implement what you've learned.

I know that you can do this. You have the method; now it's your job to dodge the shiny objects on your way to operating in your Kinetic Domain and scaling to seven figures and beyond.

ACKNOWLEDGMENTS

This book wouldn't have happened without some important people whom I'd like to take this moment to thank and acknowledge. Most important are my cats—just kidding!

Most important is Yves, my handsome husband and partner. None of this would have been possible without your constant love and support.

Mum and Dad and Jeff, your constant support means everything to me. Thank you for letting us rent your loft to do the first version of The Listings Lab live, which was the start of everything this book is about.

Dolce and Lilah, you are my grummies, and I love you for always being around—sometimes literally fluffing your tails in front of my camera mid-Zoom meeting.

Ashley, the other love of my life, you are one of my favorite humans, and I massively appreciate you. You make sure that the team and all of our members (and me!) are moving forward and turning into the best versions of ourselves.

To the entire TLL team, I could not ask for better people to be supporting our members; I'm proud to work alongside you. Every day, you take the vision and run with it. Thank you, thank you, thank you.

Zion and Alex, your mentorship, tough love, and advice have kept me going; I adore you both.

John, Ronnie, Libby, Anna, and the rest of the Lioncrest Publishing team—this has been an incredible journey that literally wouldn't have been possible without you.

Dennise, you are my favorite. I don't know what I would do without your friendship.

And to each and every single one of our members, you are all phenomenal humans, and it is the privilege and honor of a lifetime to be able to support your growth.

ABOUT THE AUTHOR

Jess Lenouvel founded The Listings Lab to help other real estate agents implement life-changing business strategies. In an age where algorithms rule our lives, her innovative approach bucks the traditional real estate mold and gives agents back their time and freedom without sacrificing growth or peace of mind. With an emphasis on marketing, personal connection, and timeless principles, Jess is a thought leader in the industry, enabling real estate agents to thrive in both their professional and personal lives.

Made in the USA
Las Vegas, NV
21 June 2022

50518884R00113